Becoming the Church People Choose

Charting New Church Courses for Relationships, Discipleship & Leadership

KAY KOTAN & KELLY COLLINS

Becoming the Church People Choose

Charting New Church Courses for Relationships, Discipleship & Leadership

books@marketsquarebooks.com
141 N. Martinwood, Suite 2 Knoxville, Tennessee 37923

ISBN: 978-1-950899-99-9

Printed and Bound in the United States of America

Editor: Sheri Carder Hood

Cover Design: Kevin Slimp

Page Design: Ashley Burton

Scripture quotations used with permission from:

Contents

INTRODUCTION

Like Ships at Sea

The ship untied from the pier and headed out of the port for a beautiful day on the water. The solo captain on board was excited for the voyage and looking forward to enjoying the sunshine and smooth ocean waves. The temperature was optimal, and the ship's accommodations were quite comfortable.

A couple of hours into the voyage, seemingly from out of nowhere, clouds move in. The sea became a bit rough, and the ocean spray began to collect on the deck of the ship. The skies grew darker. As the waves grew bigger and more frequent, the vessel began to rock back and forth, and the nose dipped further into the water. While the captain was experienced, she had never had to navigate anything quite like this derecho storm. Needless to say, this captain was fearful. She was all alone at sea, fighting an unforecasted storm without a skipper or crew. The port was no longer in sight. The beam of the lighthouse was dim at best and appeared to be a million miles away. The captain grew more anxious, afraid, helpless, and hopeless, and the waves crashed harder onto the ship's deck.

How many times have you found yourself adrift, a lone vessel upon the unforgiving seas of life? Has your heart ever run aground, helpless and hopeless, while aid was a distant harbor on the horizon? Have you experienced feeling like a ship without a rudder, unable to chart a course through the tempest, with no lighthouse in sight to pierce the darkness?

Often, assistance is just a phone call or a hand's reach away.

Yet, in those turbulent times, we sometimes mistakenly feel guilty or unworthy of help. Other times, we don't want to bother or burden anyone with the turbulent storms in our lives. Instead, we stay adrift at sea alone, in the dark, trying to navigate life on our own without a map, compass, or proper provisions. Or we naively think the storm will eventually pass on its own, and we can continue on the course to which we've become accustomed—the way we've always done it.

In our post-COVID, postmodern world, relational and mental health struggles have profoundly impacted the lives of individuals, families, the economy, the workplace, and the culture. The navigation to safe harbors is deemed too strenuous. The lighthouse is unseen, and its purpose to guide ships into a safe port remains unknown.

We are living in an unprecedented time when more people report feeling lonely, anxious, and depressed. At the same time, the majority of churches are in decline and struggling to keep their doors open. In fact, according to the predictions of Thom Rainer,[1] 15,000 churches are expected to close in 2025, and another 15,000 will no longer be able to afford a full-time pastor. At the very moment the church is called to be a beacon of hope, it is instead adrift, lacking the resources and capacity to help those in the deepening darkness.

The church is intended to be a port of call for relation*ships,* disciple*ship,* and leader*ship.* It is to be a safe harbor for equipping, resourcing, rest, and providing community for life's sailors. We were created to be in relation*ship* with one another. From the beginning, God created companionship for humankind:

---

1 Thom Rainer, "Five Reasons Why 2025 Will Be a Pivotal Year for Many Churches," *Baptist Courier,* January 27, 2025, https://baptistcourier.com/2025/01/five-reasons-why-2025-will-be-pivotal-year-for-many-churches/.

God said, "It's not good for the Man to be alone;
I'll make him a helper, a companion."

Genesis 2:18 (MSG)

Being in relation*ships* with others provides people opportunities to do life together and share life through all its seasons: the joys, celebrations, storms, struggles, crises, disappointments, deaths, illnesses, births, weddings, and more.

It's better to have a partner than go it alone.
Share the work, share the wealth.
And if one falls down, the other helps,
But if there's no one to help, tough!
Two in a bed warm each other.
Alone, you shiver all night.
By yourself, you're unprotected.
With a friend, you can face the worst.
Can you round up a third?
A three-stranded rope isn't easily snapped.

Ecclesiastes 4:10-12 (MSG)

While our society is more connected (via technology) than ever, there is a profound relation*ship* crisis. The upswing of the relation*ship* crisis was already present before the pandemic, and the isolation during COVID-19 greatly exacerbated the issue. The mental health crisis is deeply seated in relational gaps and misperceptions. More people learn and work remotely, which only adds more isolation and less human interaction.

Amid the canyon of relational gaps lies the desire for churches to reach people, but they struggle to do so amid distrust, along with the perceived judgment and hypocrisy of churches and their leaders. While there are always exceptions, the Malphurs Group estimates 80 to 85 percent of churches in

America are declining or stagnant.[2] Other resources indicate that two-thirds or more of churches are in decline. Regardless of the statistics, we can all admit that the majority of churches in the U.S. are struggling to reach new people, maintain their facilities, and meet their growing financial needs—let alone serve as the port of call for relation*ships,* disciple*ship*, and leader*ship.*

We could point to a variety of reasons for the decline, such as aging clergy, churches becoming more inwardly focused, a lack of relevance, excessive bureaucracy, a loss of missional focus, and a lack of flexibility and adaptability, to name a few. However, the decline is not the focus of this resource. While we will provide background information and state current realities as needed throughout the book, we invite you and other church leaders to view what the church of tomorrow could be. We invite you to rethink the church. We invite you to reimagine disciple*ship.* We invite you to take a journey with us in these "ships": relation*ships,* disciple*ship,* and leader*ship.*

We will explore a multitude of thoughts, ideas, and strategies that invite you to imagine the church as a safe port or harbor, guided by the lighthouse. The port is a central, stable hub where ships can dock. The port provides everything a ship needs—supplies, maintenance, and a community of other sailors. The port's purpose is to support and equip the ships for their voyages.

The ship represents a person and her life's journey. Each ship has its unique destination and purpose, but it relies on the port for preparation and support (relation*ships,* disciple*ship,* and leader*ship).* A ship's voyage is its faith, or disciple*ship* journey, and it needs to regularly return to the port to stay on course.

Just as a lighthouse provides a steady, unwavering light

---

2 "The State of the American Church: Plateaued or Declining," Malphurs Group, accessed November 15, 2025, https://malphursgroup.com/state-of-the-american-church-plateaued-declining/.

to guide ships safely to and from the port and warns them of dangers, Jesus provides the unchanging truth and direction for believers. Jesus helps ships (people) navigate their journeys, avoid spiritual hazards, and find their way to the port (the church or spiritual community) for rest and community. The lighthouse's beam cuts through the darkness, symbolizing how Jesus' teachings illuminate our paths and keep our orbits true.

An orbit represents the continuous, cyclical relation*ship* a ship has with the port, various people, and the journey of life itself. Instead of a single destination, a ship's journey is a continuous cycle of leaving port and returning. The orbit represents one's spiritual, personal, and leader*ship* development. It represents interactions with other people, including family, friends, neighbors, coaches, mentors, and spiritual directors. The ship doesn't leave the lighthouse and the port never to return. The lighthouse exerts a gravitational pull on ships, drawing them back to port. The routes inside the various orbits symbolize the charted course for the formation of the ships—relation*ships,* disciple*ship,* and leader*ship.* They signify the ongoing relation*ship* of a believer with the lighthouse and the church—a constant cycle of going out into the world (the voyage) and returning to the lighthouse and the spiritual community for teaching, equipping, and spiritual refueling (the port).

Often, ports serve as meeting points where supplies, resources, and people are delivered or picked up. A port is a meeting place, a place of connection, a place to provide or receive information, or a dispatch location.

In the early days of the U.S. church, the church owned no property. Worship took place in the community's town hall (meetinghouse). It was a natural place for people to come together, as it was the hub (harbor) of community life. The town hall was used throughout the week for town meetings and public gatherings of all types—political, social, and economic life of the town. But soon, the church felt the secular and sacred needed separating, so it began building its own "sacred spaces" and banned what it deemed too political or too "rowdy."[3] Rather than continuing to meet at the epicenter of the community, this move began the ever-growing separation of the church from the everyday life and influence of its community. The meetinghouse enabled the church to be part of the town's "port," where people came together and were then dispatched once again into the community. When the church became separate from the town's harbor, the building of relation*ships* became more difficult. The chasm between the town harbor and the church has widened and grown ever since.

Imagine if the church once again became a harbor—a port of call for relation*ships,* disciple*ship*, and leader*ship.* Imagine the church as the epicenter of your community once again, where everyone feels comfortable and welcome. Imagine the church as a place where people's orbits intersect with others in meaningful, life-giving ways—not just for an hour on Sunday morning. Imagine the church as a place where people find valuable and needed resources to sustain basic life or to improve their life's journey. Imagine the church as the first place people turn for comfort, counsel, assurance, care, guidance, grace, prayer, and forgiveness.

We believe it is possible to build and capture this kind of community culture once again. But, friends, it will take those of us steeped in the traditions of the church we have grown accustomed to and are comfortable with to view the church of tomorrow in a different light. It will take us reimagining what

---

[3] Kenda Creasy Dean, *Innovating for Love: Joining God's Expedition Through Christian Social Innovation,* vol. 23, The Greatest Expedition series (Market Square Books, 2022).

it means to be the church (harbor) that people want and need. It will take us being so brokenhearted for those who don't yet have a relation*ship* with Jesus Christ to become less self-focused and more centered on the Great Commission and the Great Commandment, as Jesus instructed. It will take us focusing on the ships—relation*ships,* disciple*ship,* and leader*ship.*

The church of today is what the congregants have made it. Most of the doings and goings-on of any given church are not sacred. It is what the people have interpreted or decided a church should be and do. And let's be honest, for the most part, it is not working well. The church is struggling to be faithful to its call and purpose. The church is losing more relevance and effectiveness year after year. With a sense of urgency, it is time for us to peel back the curtain, take a hard look at our ministries, and reimagine the church in ways that will truly reach new people. While the journey will likely not be easy (and perhaps stormy), it will be simpler. Focus on one thing and one thing only—all the ships: relation*ship,* disciple*ship,* and leader*ship.*

When the ships become the focus, the rest of the details will take care of themselves.

In our postmodern, post-Christian world, the lay of the land has dramatically changed. The winds of the seas have shifted. The needs and desires of people (relation*ships)* have evolved. To become or stay a preferred port of call, a church will need to become increasingly adaptable, flexible, culturally competent, and mature in disciple*ship.* In addition, to be the preferred port of call, relation*ships,* disciple*ship,* and leader*ship* must be the key drivers and focus.

If a church feels called to become a preferred orbital port of call, its current charted course will need to be adjusted. Let's incorporate the essentials in this resource and identify the key elements to launch and chart a new course for your church.

Christ the Lighthouse

Every harbor needs a fixed point of reference, a beacon that never shifts. For the church, Christ is the Lighthouse—the un-

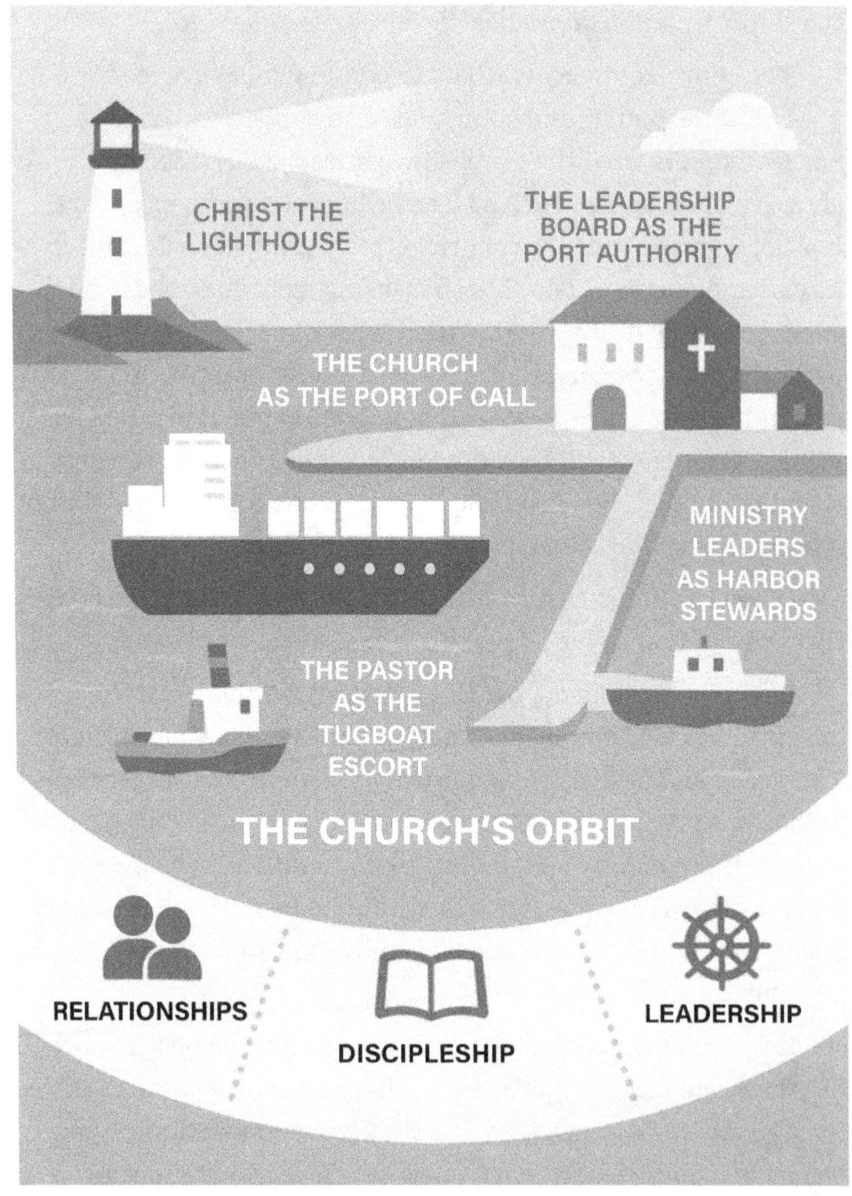

wavering light that guides every (relation, disciple, and leader) *ship* safely toward the shore. The lighthouse does not move with the waves, nor does it depend on the weather. It simply shines. For the church, Christ is that steady presence, ensuring that all navigation begins and ends with Jesus. Without the lighthouse, ships wander blindly. With Christ, the destination is clear: life in Christ and mission through Christ.

The Holy Spirit as the Undercurrent

Just as an ocean's undercurrent, the Holy Spirit is independent of surface currents and flows strongly beneath them. Like the undercurrent, the Holy Spirit is not visible but always at work. Undercurrents are often produced by disturbances such as debris, rocks, bridge pilings, and ships. The Holy Spirit is always present through the calm and the disturbances—sight unseen.

The Church as the Port of Call

If Christ is the Lighthouse, then the church is the port of call—the place where (relation, disciple, and leader)*ships* find refuge, repair, and resupply before heading back to sea. A port is never the end of the journey; it is the stopping point where vessels are restored for a greater purpose. Likewise, the church exists not only to gather people in safety but, even more importantly, to prepare (relation, disciple, and leader) ships to sail again into the world with the Good News.

Ports of call are also called harbors. Harbors typically have a natural or manufactured protection called a breakwater. A breakwater around their entry protects the harbor from waves and currents.

Inside harbors, there are piers. Piers are raised structures extending over water, typically supported on pilings, and are used for various purposes such as walking, fishing, sightseeing, and providing deep-water access for boats or ships. Ships tie up to piers to keep them from floating back out to sea and to allow access for loading or unloading cargo and for people to embark and disembark.

Tucked inside the harbor alongside businesses and homes, the church is not the only building in a port of call. It's important to remember that the church is no longer the center of culture nor the harbor. Today's church is countercultural—but not always in a positive way. For the church to become a preferred port of call, it will need to become a safe place to refuel, train, and rest. Ships will need resources from the church, and in turn, the church will send the ships out once again for their continued journey.

A port is designed for movement. Ships come in, but they also must go out. If they only ever stay in the harbor, they stagnate. A healthy church, like a healthy port, ensures flow: receiving people in, building them up, and sending them out. Optimally, the church becomes the preferred port of call for all *ships* (relation, disciple, and leader) near your harbor.

The Pastor as the Tugboat Escort

Ships (people) may be large and impressive, but they cannot maneuver into or out of a harbor alone. They need guidance and support. This is where the pastor, as the tugboat escort, comes in. The tugboat escort is smaller but immensely strong, uniquely designed to guide *ships* (relation, disciple, and leader) through narrow channels, around obstacles, and toward the correct berth.

A pastor does the same. Pastors escort people into the life of the church, ensuring they dock where they can be nourished. They also escort people back out, reminding them that the mission is not in the harbor but on the open seas of everyday life. The tugboat escort does not overshadow the ships; rather, it enables the ships to fulfill their purpose.

Ministry Leaders as Harbor Stewards

Ports only function well when harbor stewards are well-equipped and in place, ready to respond. Harbor stewards are the ministry leaders, those who ensure that every dock is maintained, every warehouse is stocked, and every ship is cared for. Harbor stewards create the systems of support—hospitality, teaching, service, evangelism, discipling opportunities—that allow ships to find exactly what they need for the journey ahead.

Harbor stewards may not be as visible as the escort tugboat, but without their attentiveness, the port would collapse into disorder. They embody servant leader*ship*, providing both structure and care.

The Leader*ship* Board as the Port Authority

Every port has a governing body: the port authority. In the church, the port authority is the leader*ship* board. Their responsibility is not to run every detail of the harbor but to ensure the mission remains aligned, resources are stewarded wisely, and operations remain accountable.

The port authority sets policies, grants permissions, and ensures safety. In the church context, they guard against mission drift, hold leaders accountable, and keep the focus on Christ the Lighthouse. Without the port authority, a port risks becoming chaotic, vulnerable, or misaligned with its true purpose.

(Relation, Disciple, and Leader)ships as God's People

The ships themselves are the people who come into the harbor. Each ship carries unique cargo—gifts, talents, experiences, and callings. Each also requires care, repair, and direction. Ships differ in size and type. Some are small fishing boats; others are mighty cargo carriers. Yet all are valued and serve a unique purpose in the seas of life.

Ships are never meant to stay docked permanently. They are built for movement. They are made for a special purpose. In the church, people are prepared not just for safety but for mission. A ship tied to the dock forever becomes rusty and useless; a disciple who never ventures into the world fails to live out their calling. Fleets are made up of countless ships, just like people are meant to be in relation*ships* with countless others. Without leader*ship*, a port of call will fall into disrepair physically, spiritually, and financially.

The Church's Orbit

Just as each ship has its orbit, so does the port itself. The church's orbit is not a random circling of activity but intentional pathways that ensure growth and mission. This orbit has three essential tracks: building relation*ships*, the disciple*ship* pathway, and the leader*ship* pathway.

The Orbits of Ships: Activities and Disciple*ship*

As ships sail, they trace orbits, patterns of travel, and purpose. For people, these orbits are their daily activities and disciple*ship* practices. Each orbit reveals where its time and energy are invested, whether in relation*ships*, disciple*ship*, or leader*ship*. The question is not whether people orbit, but whether their orbits are aligned with the port of call's (church) true mission (making disciples who transform the world), guided by the Lighthouse (Christ). A church's orbit needs to prepare, influence, and form a ship's orbit. The ship's orbits then intersect, influence, and shape other ships' orbits.

When ships and their respective orbits drift from the lighthouse's bright beam of light, ships risk getting lost. But when disciple*ship* forms one's orbit, people remain anchored in Christ while moving purposefully outward into new relation*ships*.

The Disciple*ship* Orbit

Both the church and the ships' orbits represent the disciple*ship* development—the intentional pathways that guide people from curious seekers to fully engaged disciples. This pathway charts a movement inward for growth and outward for mission, keeping the harbor's rhythm healthy and sustainable. This movement within the disciple*ship* pathway deepens people's faith, aligns them with Christ the Lighthouse, and grounds them in scripture, prayer, and spiritual practices.

Without a clear pathway, ships might wander aimlessly in circles or dock without purpose. But with it, the harbor becomes a place of transformation: ships are continually strengthened and continually sent.

The Leader*ship* Orbit

Just as the disciple*ship* orbit forms people spiritually, the leader*ship* orbit develops and multiplies those who will guide and develop others. Without intentional leader*ship* formation, work in the harbor (church) eventually stalls. Ships may continue to arrive, but no escort tugboats, harbor stewards, or port authorities will be prepared or present to guide them.

The purpose of the leader*ship* development pathway is sustainability—to ensure the harbor never depends on a single escort tugboat (pastor) or a few harbor stewards. It also ensures multiplication by equipping new leaders to step into roles, expanding the harbor's capacity. Finally, leader*ship* development ensures Kingdom reach by developing strong leaders who escort more ships in and out, resulting in greater missional impact. The key elements of leader*ship* development are identification, invitation, equipping, deploying, and multiplying. Leader*ship* cannot exist apart from disciple*ship*. Together, they form a pathway that ensures leaders are not only competent but also spiritually grounded.

The two orbits are concentric, overlapping, and interdependent:

- **Disciple*ship* forms the heart** (Christlike character).
- **Leader*ship* equips the hands** (skills and responsibilities).

Together, disciple*ship* and leader*ship* create a dual orbit: one that nurtures spiritual maturity and another that multiplies capacity. When a church aligns these orbits, it prevents ships from circling aimlessly. Instead, every vessel grows inward in Christlikeness and outward in influence, strengthening both the harbor and the seas beyond. And finally, relation*ships* weave into both the disciple*ship* and the leader*ship* orbits. These three ships are foundational vessels that anchor the port in its purpose.

The Three Ships: Relation*ships,* Disciple*ship,* and Leader*ship*

All of this rests on these **three core ships:**

1. **Relation*ships*** – Every ship depends on connection. Harbors exist because people are meant to travel together, not alone. Relation*ships* provide a sense of belonging, encouragement, and accountability.
2. **Disciple*ship*** – This is the cargo every ship must carry. A vessel without cargo is empty; a Christian without disciple*ship* is hollow. Disciple*ship* is the equipping

process that fills ships with what the world truly needs.

3. **Leader*ship*** – No fleet thrives without port authorities, harbor stewards, and escort tugboats. Leader*ship* multiplies the harbor's capacity and enables more ships to sail effectively.

These three ships form the heartbeat of a missional church: an orbital port. When they move and weave together—relation*ships* for belonging, disciple*ship* for growth, leader*ship* for guidance—the port thrives and the seas beyond are impacted—all of which are guided by the bright beam of the Lighthouse.

To recap, here are the elements of the orbital port:

Christ the Lighthouse	A fixed point outside the harbor guiding all ships
The Undercurrent	The Holy Spirit
Church as Port of Call (Harbor)	The hub of the harbor's activity: relation*ship*, disciple*ship*, and leader*ship* for inviting, equipping, and deploying
Pastor as the Escort Tugboat	Guiding ships (people) into and out of the harbor
Ministry Leaders as Harbor Stewards	Managing docks, recruiting and equipping disciples, coordinating, assessing, and ensuring care
Leader*ship* Board as Port Authority	Governing missional alignment
Ships as People	Entering for renewal, leaving for mission, each with their own personal orbit (daily spiritual practices of disciple*ship*, leader*ship*, relation*ships*, and other activities)
Church's Orbit	The energy and intentionality surrounding the harbor and its mission

Disciple*ship* Orbit	Spiritual formation, maturity, and multiplication that are woven into the church's and the ships' orbits
Leader*ship* Orbit	Growing and equipping new and existing leaders that are woven into the church's and the ships' orbits
Growing Relation*ships*	Woven into personal and port's orbits with intentional Christlikeness

The church as a port of call is not a static place of safety but a dynamic hub of movement, growth, and multiplication. Christ the Lighthouse is the unchanging guide. The pastor, as the tugboat, escorts people in and out with strength and care. Ministry leaders steward the harbor; the board governs as the port authority; and the people—ships of many kinds—find renewal before being sent out again to sea.

The orbits of individual lives and the orbit of the port ensure alignment, intentionality, and momentum for key investments in these three essential ships—**relation*ships*, disciple*ship*, and leader*ship***—which together make the harbor a launching ground for Kingdom impact across the seas.

Now that you have the lay of the land (or maybe gained your sea legs), are you ready? Let's begin this shared journey of envisioning your church as a port of call lit by the lighthouse to equip the ships—where missionally focused relation*ships*, disciple*ship*, and leader*ship* take root and new people join you in a transformative walk with Jesus Christ. So pack your bags (and yes, even your baggage), and let's navigate the seas together, side by side.

CHAPTER ONE

The Crisis of Relationships

My dear, dear friends, if God loved us like this,
we certainly ought to love each other.
No one has seen God, ever.
But if we love one another,
God dwells deeply within us,
and his love becomes complete in us—perfect love!

1 John 4:11-12 (MSG)

As we chart our life courses and desired destinations, relation*ships* make up a great deal of our life (our ship) decisions, hopes, dreams, plans, and intentions. Those relation*ships*, such as parents, siblings, extended family, friends, life partners, neighbors, mentors, spiritual leaders, and co-workers, can all have profound impacts on your formation and views (your orbits and their connections to relation*ships*, disciple*ship*, and leader*ship*). It is those very orbits (life's intentional and unintentional voyages) of our ship/life that profoundly shape our lives, especially our relation*ships*, disciple*ship*, and leader*ship*.

At one time, the church was not only the preferred port of call but also provided training for the ship's crew: the ship's captains, first mates, and crew. The church also equipped the ship's crew on how to navigate the waters, weather the storms, use a compass properly, chart a course, understand proper terminology, use the ship's architecture, and more. It used to be the leading community change-makers and caretakers, a welcoming, loving place to be, to land, explore, serve, and grow. The church used to be the one that built hospitals when people didn't have the care they needed and the one that built schools and colleges to provide more learning opportunities for a broader span of people.

While the light from the Lighthouse (Christ) has never dimmed, the church is no longer the preferred port of call for most ships. The church has turned inward and is no longer relevant or needed by the ships. The church struggles to provide instruction, formation, or transformation for relation*ship,* disciple*ship*, and leader*ship.*

This chapter is chock-full of data and statistics. Please do not allow the extensive use of numbers to dissuade you from digging in, and please don't skip or disregard this important foundation upon which the rest of the book sits. These statistics are shared to substantiate the needs and the crisis level and to provide leaders with vital information rather than simply our thoughts and feelings. As a church leader, you may want to share these important statistics with other leaders and your congregation to help overcome any reluctance or doubts as you invite them to re-envision what the church may need to look like in the near future.

In this chapter, we will explore specific demographic groups (different types of *ships/people)* in which a lack of relation*ships,* connections, and a sense of community (limited or interrupted orbits and disconnection from the port and lighthouse) tell the stories of the church's relation*ship* crisis. While many other ships (people) could also be included, we'll focus on how the relation*ship* crisis has hindered the church's ability to build meaningful connections—especially with those facing mental health challenges, young adults, moms, Gen Z, and the "Nones."

Time for a Shipshape Church

Too often, we (Christians and the church) shy away from "touchy subjects" or topics that might be "too controversial" for a church setting. We often find it easier to ignore the church decline and its growing irrelevance and distance from young adults, mothers of young children, and those struggling with mental health than to address it. Facing reality—and the circumstances that come with it—is often too difficult. As a result, the church ends up celebrating busyness instead of pursuing impact and transformation. If a church chooses to dive in and have a positive impact on any one of these demographics, it will likely need to make some difficult choices and changes that will cause some congregational discomfort. For many churches, the ongoing comfort of the existing remnant congregation has become the leading criterion for decision-making.

As we circle back to the introductory nautical metaphor, the current landscape suggests the church is ignoring the mayday calls of those ships that have run aground and those that are adrift. The ships that now encounter storms and rough seas can no longer find refuge, refueling, camaraderie, supplies, or training that they had once found in the port of call (the church). The church no longer offers assistance in charting courses to prepare the ships' crews for those intentional orbits of life at sea.

No two ships have the same destinations or voyage experiences, just as one person's life is uniquely different from any other. Those life/ship journeys are shaped by the training and formation, the interactions with others, and the influence of other ships and their voyages. In other words, each person/ship has these intentional or unintentional "orbits" that interact with one's life/ship and the resulting voyages and destinations.

We will now begin to dive deeper into the church's opportunities and responsibilities for investing in and caring for the ships (people) and their voyages (orbits) in their harbor (mission field). As stated earlier, we will concentrate on some specific kinds of ships—such as moms, young adults, and the Nones—and on one specific orbit: mental health. We chose these specific areas to explore and highlight for leaders because they closely relate to the church's mission, the large percentages of people who make up these demographics, and the enormous potential impact the church could have if it were to invest in just one of them.

How the Relation*ship* Crisis Impacts Mental Health

It is no secret that our country feels deeply divided on so many levels. In a 2024 survey, Ipsos reported that 81 percent of Americans say America is more divided than united, and 78 percent say the country is less united than it was ten years ago. Interestingly, only 24 percent say that religious leaders are helping to bring the country together, while 36 percent say religious leaders are increasing the division. Yet, 69 percent say that most Americans want the same things out of life.[4]

If seven out of ten Americans believe most Americans want the same things from life, it is curious to consider why there is such division. In a *Harvard Gazette* article, Robert Putnam, author of *Bowling Alone* and *The Upswing,* explains his belief that the divide is "all due to a growing lack of social connection, and it's visible in our relation*ships,* communities, and deeply riven politics." Putnam further explains that "what we have to do is connect. Rebuild those social networks that allowed Americans to interact across class and education

[4] "Americans view country as deeply divided, but believe most have much in common," Ipsos, April 29, 2024, https://www.ipsos.com/en-us/with-honor-ipsos.

lines." Ultimately, he says, "It is absolutely crucial that this new movement be based on youth. There are cultural things that young people of any class can bond on."[5]

In an article from *Psychology Today,* the impact of divisiveness on mental health is addressed, and notes the critical need for people to reconnect lovingly:

> *These dynamics (prolonged political divisiveness and high-functioning depression) interact to deepen emotional burnout by compounding feelings of isolation and chronic stress in a politically charged environment.*
>
> *To combat this, we must collectively promote empathy over argumentation. Challenges like bridging the divide between different belief systems or fostering mutual understanding among diverse political affiliations can feel Herculean. Yet, every empathetic conversation, shared moment of vulnerability, and effort to understand rather than contradict adds a ripple of change.*
>
> *When neighbors speak to one another with respect, when families choose to debate lovingly rather than adversarially, and when communities elevate tolerance above reactionary criticism, the result is gradual healing—not just for the individual, but for the society they inhabit.*[6]

As Christians, our faith is grounded in hope, peace, joy, and love. Yet the news feeds are full of stories detailing the depression, loneliness, anxiety, and stress tied to the national

---

5 Clea Simon, "Want a Less Divisive America? Just a Matter of Trust," *Harvard Gazette,* March 14, 2025, https://news.harvard.edu/gazette/story/2025/03/want-a-less-divisive-american-just-a-matter-of-trust/.

6 Judith Joseph, M.D., "When Politics and the Mind Collide," *Psychology Today* (blog: Navigating High-Functioning Mental Health Conditions), January 31, 2025, https://www.psychologytoday.com/us/blog/navigating-high-functioning-mental-health-conditions/202501/when-politics-and-the-mind-collide.

mental health crisis. As Christians, we have to wonder where the church is (and could be) in the midst of this crisis.

The statistics are staggering—such as 41 percent of the 76,000 surveyed college students reported symptoms of depression, and 36 percent experienced anxiety. Nearly 50,000 people died by suicide in the U.S. in 2022 (up 2.6 percent from 2021), and there was a 40 percent increase from 2009 to 2019 in the number of high school students who reported persistent feelings of sadness or hopelessness.[7]

The Zebra[8] report on mental health statistics from 2024 identifies some of these key insights:

- 1 in 5 Americans suffers from a mental illness (National Institute of Mental Health).
- 40 million Americans suffer from anxiety (Anxiety and Depression Association of America).
- In 2024, an estimated 57.8 million adults (19% of the country) had a mental illness, but only 43% received any kind of mental health care.
- Suicide is the 10th leading cause of death in the United States.
- 20% of all teens suffer from depression before they reach adulthood.
- Teen depression has increased 59% since 2007.
- Those teens who suffer from depression also have a 30% chance of developing a drug problem later in life.
- About 30% of active-duty and military personnel deployed

---

[7] Jen Christensen, "The U.S. Has a Mental Health Crisis That Could Undermine Our Democracy, U.S. Surgeons General Say," *CNN*, September 28, 2023, https://www.cnn.com/2023/09/28/health/mental-health-crisis-undermine-our-democracy-us-surgeon-generals-say/index.html.

[8] The Zebra, "Mental Health Statistics," July 26, 2024, https://www.thezebra.com/resources/research/mental-health-statistics/.

in Iraq and Afghanistan suffer from mental illness.

- Over 40% of all veterans struggle with their mental health or substance abuse.
- Over 20% of veterans return home with Traumatic Brain Injury and PTSD.
- A little over 77% of service members in active duty hospitalized for Post-Traumatic Stress Disorder have comorbidities.

We are called to love God with our whole heart, mind, and soul, and love our neighbor as ourselves (Matthew 22:37). Just as Christ loves, one can't turn a blind eye to this crisis. As Wesleyan people, we are called to pursue a life of social holiness, to love those we encounter throughout our life's voyage. God created us to be relational beings, to be in relation*ships*, to be social, and to be in community with one another. Therefore, as disciples of Christ, as neighbors to those who are hurting, and as people who call ourselves Wesleyans, we must be agents of social holiness. John Wesley wrote, "Solitary religion is not to be found there. 'Holy Solitaries' is a phrase no more consistent with the gospel than Holy Adulterers. The gospel of Christ knows of no religion, but social; no holiness but social holiness. Faith working by love, is the length and breadth and depth and height of Christian perfection."[9]

Connecting Relation*ships* and Mental Health Orbits

What role can your local church play in overcoming the mental health crisis? How can you, as a Christian, help just one person struggling with mental health? No community is immune to the effects of this crisis. As agents of social holiness, we, as the church and as disciples of Jesus, must help find

[9] John Wesley, *Hymns and Sacred Poems* (London: 1739), preface, viii.

solutions and offer hope and love to our neighbors suffering from mental illness.

We are not naive enough to believe that the church has all the answers. We all know the church is not a professional healthcare facility. But we can be the convener of conversations. We can offer community. We can offer love, support, and hope. We can partner with other mental health care providers in our community to leverage their work for the greater good and impact.

Dr. Jerome Adams, U.S. Surgeon General from 2017-2021, argued that the country can't completely treat its way out of the problem (the mental health crisis) "since only 20% of health is actually addressed in a doctor's office. The rest of what impacts human health, including mental health, is what happens in communities. The other 80% happens in communities that are connected, that are supportive of women and minorities, that have childcare, that have good educational opportunities, that have a good-paying job, or both. And I think we need to really focus on building those stronger communities."[10]

Wow! Take a moment to read Dr. Adams' statement again. Let his message soak in. So often, we believe there is nothing the church can do to address the mental health crisis. But according to Adams, the church as a whole and we as individual disciples can have a profound impact on 80 percent of health outcomes! Doesn't the needed community Adams describes sound exactly like the kind of community the church is meant to be? Maybe the church isn't always as Adams described, but even if the church were 75 percent or even half that kind of community, imagine the positive impact the church could have on reversing this mental health crisis! A sense of connection through belonging is vital to our physical and mental health.

---

[10] Christensen, "Mental Health Crisis That Could Undermine Our Democracy."

Dr. Vivek Murthy, U.S. Surgeon General from 2021-2025, paints a beautiful picture of a community full of hope and love with this summary:

> *I think we're actually more grounded in the core values of kindness and generosity, of service and friendship. I think that's what we want. A world fueled by love is a world where we're kind to each other, where we're generous. It's a world where we value friendships. We heal through the love that we give and the love that we receive. And when you realize that, you realize that we're all healers, and this is a time that the world needs more healers.*[11]

Some of the top mental health challenges include depression, anxiety, isolation, and loneliness. Dr. Vivek Murthy declared a national loneliness and social isolation epidemic in 2023. Murthy says, "Loneliness is a subjective feeling—that the connections that we need in our life are greater than the connections we actually have." Murthy acknowledges the decline in participation in organizations (recreational leagues and service organizations) that has contributed to the isolation. Dr. Murthy explains:

> *We know now that when people struggle with things socially disconnected, over time, that it can have an impact on their mental health, increasing their risk for anxiety and depression, but also on their physical health, increasing their risk for heart disease, as well as dementia and premature death. The overall mortality impact of loneliness and isolation is on par with smoking daily, and they're even greater than the mortality impact we see with obesity.*[12]

In reporting on data collected from the Household Pulse

---

11 Christensen, "Mental Health Crisis That Could Undermine Our Democracy."

12 Youri Benadjaoud, "U.S. Surgeon General Warns of Dangers of Loneliness," *ABC News*, June 12, 2024, https://abcnews.go.com/Health/us-surgeon-general-warns-dangers-loneliness/story?id=111050040.

Survey, Ryan Burge, research director at My Faith Counts, former pastor, associate professor at Eastern Illinois University, and writer at Graphs About Religion, shared insights into the socialization patterns of various generations. This is the question asked of the survey participants: "How often do you get together with friends or relatives on a weekly basis?"

Which generation would you guess gathered with others most often? Least often? The results might surprise you. Gen X reported the highest percentage (45 percent) of not gathering with friends and relatives at all, followed by Millennials at 44 percent. The Silent Generation reported the highest participation rate (14 percent) in gatherings five or more times a week, followed by the Boomers at 10 percent. Gen Z reported the highest percentage (17 percent) of gathering three or four times per week, followed by the Silent Generation and Boomers with 16 percent each. These statistics indicate that Gen X and Millennials are the least social, and the Silent Generation, Boomers, and Gen Z are more social.[13]

Murthy offers this simple "five for five connection" to help people begin to connect with one another:

It involves making one active connection each day for the next five days. That could be expressing gratitude to someone. It could be calling a friend to extend help to them at a time when they're struggling. Or it could be asking for help yourself. But doing this over five days will make you feel different. And my hope is that that will be a jumping off point to help people build these kinds of practices into their life for the long term.[14]

Besides a sense of belonging, community offers people

---

[13] Ryan Burge, "Are People Really Lonely and Miserable," Graphs About Religion, September 2, 2024, 2025, https://www.graphsaboutreligion.com/p/are-people-really-lonely-and-miserable.

[14] Benadjaoud, "U.S. Surgeon General Warns of Dangers of Loneliness."

the opportunity to find meaning in their lives and to make a difference in the world. When the culture was more church-centric, these human needs for social connection, self-worth, and self-realization were often met in the church. While some still find this in a church community, most have found it in other places (spiritual communities, sports leagues, nonprofit organizations, etc.). Yet, as the statistics indicate, the great majority of people still feel disconnected and long for a sense of belonging, purpose, and impact.[15]

There is a great need and opportunity for the church to be a source of community for its neighbors. However, an attractional approach (the desire and expectation that people will come to the church, primarily on Sunday morning) for building community is not effective. Rather, an approach to building authentic relation*ships* out in the community (harbor) is needed. This approach of sending out and being in the community returns us to the basics.

Genuinely investing in new relation*ships* is key. Focusing on the endgame of a new friend becoming a new church member is not the recommended approach. Instead, a focus on building an authentic relation*ship,* where one truly cares about the person and wants the best for them, is more desirable. The opportunity to share about your faith will naturally evolve authentically over time from a sense of curiosity and the desire to know and trust one another more deeply.

General Surgeons Adams and Murthy, both acclaimed medical doctors, proclaim the monumental impact a loving community can have on addressing and overcoming the mental health crisis in our country. What kind of loving community is your church providing for those suffering from mental health

15 Benadjaoud, "U.S. Surgeon General Warns of Dangers of Loneliness."

illnesses? How might this quote from Mother Teresa help frame the kind of community your church might create?

To love another person is to touch the face of God.
It is possible to give without loving,
but it is impossible to love without giving.

Mother Teresa

Connecting Relation*ships* and the Crisis Impacting Moms

In Barna's Mother's Day edition of *Stats for Sermons,*[16] the statistics speak to the overwhelming role mothers assume in the faith formation of their children. In surveying practicing Christian teens, we learn that 79 percent of their mothers encouraged them to attend church, 66 percent taught them about the Bible, and 72 percent taught them about traditions. Yet, 47 percent of mothers reported that their church never provides them with materials specifically to support them as mothers. This means nearly half the mothers who typically provide faith formation for their children are doing so without the necessary support.

Here is a summary of the data: Between 66 percent and 80 percent of the mothers surveyed lacked a community that would support them, value them, provide a positive influence, care for their children, or offer a safe place to be authentic.

The above data is not only alarming but should cause us to pause and examine our ministry approaches with moms and families! How does your church qualify as the minority exception to these survey results? Or, how will your church specifically change your ministry approach to reverse these shocking statistics?

---

[16] Barna Group, *MOPS Webinar Full Replay,* accessed December 2, 2025, https://barna.gloo.us/videos/mops-webinar-full-replay.

A survey conducted by The Ohio State University Wexner Medical Center found that two-thirds of parents who felt the demands of parenthood sometimes or frequently felt isolated and lonely! Sixty-two percent felt burned out by parental responsibilities. Thirty-eight percent felt they had no one to support them in their parenting role. Seventy-nine percent would value a way to connect with other parents outside work and home![17]

Anxiety and exhaustion are common realities for the majority of today's mothers. According to Barna's survey, 68 percent of mothers agree or somewhat agree that they feel tired most of the time. Seventy-seven percent of mothers agree or somewhat agree that they usually find themselves worrying about something.[18]

In a webinar titled "Engaging Moms: The Evangelism Strategy No One is Talking About But Should Be,"[19] Kelli Smith, MOPS director of church engagement and marketing, talks with Joe Jenson, senior vice president in content and engagement at Barna. In the webinar, Smith shares revealing research conducted in the fall of 2023. Here are some of Smith's key points:

- Mothers are evangelists who are forming the faith of the next generation.
- Mothers are disciplers, showing the next generation how to grow.

---

17 "New Survey Finds Loneliness Epidemic Runs Deep Among Parents," The Ohio State University College of Nursing, April 24, 2024, https://nursing.osu.edu/news/2024/05/01/new-survey-finds-loneliness-epidemic-runs-deep-among-parents.

18 "New Survey Finds Loneliness Epidemic Runs Deep Among Parents."

19 "Engaging Moms: The Evangelism Strategy No One Is Talking About But Should Be," accessed November 15, 2025, https://barna.gloo.us/videos/mops-webinar-full-replay.

- Mothers are underserved by the church.
- 47% of mothers said their church never provides materials specifically intended to support them as mothers.
- 52% of pastors say their church could do a better job of serving mothers.
- Fewer than half of mothers feel content and safe within their community.
- While mothers are satisfied with their relation*ships* with their children, other areas of life suffer (e.g., marriage/ romantic relation*ships,* friendships, mental health, finance, career).
- Only 19% of mothers feel they are able to meaningfully contribute to the world on a regular basis.
- Mothers feel held back and therefore pull away from the church.
- Three ways the church can better serve and shepherd mothers:
    - Ensure communities for mothers are safe, authentic, and supportive.
    - Disciple mothers holistically (support growth relationally, spiritually, emotionally, and as a parent).
    - Provide equal opportunities for mothers.

During the launch of the *Motherhood Today Podcast,*[20] Mandy Ariot, president and CEO of MomCo, and David Kinnamon, president of Barna, announced the publication of the study "Motherhood Today: The State of Moms and What It Means for the Church,"[21] a collaboration with Barna and

---

[20] "Introducing Motherhood Today Podcast," Barna, Motherhood Today Podcast, February 27, 2024, https://www.barna.com/episodes/introducing-motherhood-today-podcast/.

[21] "Motherhood Today: The State of Moms and What It Means for the Church," Barna,

MomCo (formerly MOPS). Here are some interesting and key summary points of their research and the resulting Motherhood Today report:

1. A mother's influence stretches into every sphere of life, but many moms fail to recognize their value or impact. Only 19% say they are able to contribute meaningfully to the world.

2. Many mothers (including Christian moms) don't think very highly of their community.

3. Along with gaps in the community, anxiety and exhaustion are evident in the lives of most moms.

4. Faith correlates with stronger emotional well-being among mothers.

5. Christian moms prioritize church attendance and say they do so primarily to grow their personal faith. Yet, ministries and resources for mothers are limited in churches.

6. Nearly one in four Christian moms is dissatisfied with their church.

This report offers nearly eighty pages of timely, poignant data and insights about moms, as well as articles from professionals on strategies to engage them. It is a goldmine of information to read and understand if your church has a desire to connect meaningfully with more moms and their children.

In a February 2024 Motherhood Today Podcast, Dr. Anita Phillips,[22] trauma therapist, minister, and author of *The Garden*

Motherhood Today, May 7, 2024, accessed November 15, 2025, https://www.barna.com/motherhood-today-free-digital-report/.

[22] Dr. Anita Phillips on Motherhood & Mental Health," Motherhood Today Podcast, Barna,

Within, weighed in on moms from her purview as a mom, pastor, counselor, and coach. Dr. Phillips shared that Christian statistics are very similar to secular statistics. In other words, the anxiety, exhaustion, and stress levels are no different in the churched and unchurched populations.

As a therapist, Dr. Phillips offers this definition of trauma: "an experience that overwhelms our bodies and nervous systems' capacity to absorb the experience." She cautions that unresolved trauma resurfaces when adults have not worked through the trauma to heal—especially at the time when the children reach the age at which the trauma occurred in the parent's life. This is why the healing of trauma is essential for parents, so the cycle of trauma does not repeat.

Phillips also reminds us that it is okay to feel and be emotional. It is part of being human. Interestingly, Millennials and Gen Z are more open to talking about their feelings, therapy, counseling, and mental health.

Jesus modeled feelings throughout his ministry. For example, he frequently showed compassion for the suffering, both physical and emotional. He healed the sick, comforted the grieving, and had empathy for those marginalized in society. Jesus experienced deep sadness, even to the point of sorrowful prayer in the Garden of Gethsemane. He wept over the impending destruction of Jerusalem and the death of Lazarus. While often gentle and compassionate, Jesus also displayed righteous anger, particularly when encountering hypocrisy or injustice. He cleansed the temple, overturning tables and driving out those who were exploiting others.

Jesus wasn't solely defined by sorrow or anger. He also experienced joy and celebrated with others, as seen in his

---

February 29, 2024, https://www.barna.com/episodes/2-dr-anita-phillips-on-motherhood-mental-health/.

participation in the wedding at Cana, where he turned water into wine. Jesus wasn't afraid to express his raw emotions to God in prayer. In the Garden of Gethsemane, he prayed with deep anguish and sorrow, demonstrating that it's okay to be honest with God about one's feelings. In essence, Jesus' emotional life was complex and multifaceted, reflecting the full range of human experience. He didn't shy away from difficult emotions but rather engaged with them in a way that honored God and served others. This makes him a relatable figure and a model for how Christians can navigate their own emotional lives.

As both a minister and a trauma therapist, Phillips offered some tips on how to share about mental health from the pulpit. First, she shared that translation is needed. Secondly, it's not difficult to translate from the language of scripture to the language of mental health. All that's needed is to recognize that it is all in scripture. One's beliefs, heart, mind, and behavior (mental health language) are equal to and translate to knowing, thinking, feeling, and doing (scripture language). It is important to note that the Bible talks about the heart way more than the mind. Therefore, it is important to understand that from our hearts, our thoughts grow, and from our thoughts, our behaviors come.

On the podcast, Dr. Phillips is asked how churches can orient ministries to help moms specifically with anxiety and exhaustion. She first suggested that regular support and connection opportunities are important and desired by moms. She also suggested that the church offer multiple examples of family models from the pulpit as acceptable (e.g., single parents, grandparents, aunts and uncles raising children, stay-at-home moms, working moms, and homeschooling moms). One final suggestion she offered is to have a trauma-informed approach to every conversation with families. For example, don't ask why a person did something. Instead, ask what happened to you in the past or what is happening to you now? Be curious.

Moms and women in general are also key when it comes to connecting with messages and methods relating to generosity. According to Barna's "The State of Generosity,"[23] women are key contributors and decision-makers in the landscape of generosity. In fact, 85 percent of household financial decisions are made by women/mothers. But we often miss the mark in our communication around generosity that speaks and relates to women. For example, how are stories of generous women of the Bible (e.g., Rebekah and Tabitha) woven into messaging? Women relate to generosity messaging that tends to be careful, cyclical, heartfelt, and hands-on.

Mothers have a huge impact on the home, including raising, equipping, and influencing their children and their financial decisions. Yet too many moms feel disconnected, undervalued, unsupported, and unable to influence their communities (including churches). Without moms, the church will not have children. How is your church bridging this gap?

Connecting Relation*ships* and the Crisis Impacting Youth and Young Adults

The majority of churches struggle to reach youth and young adults. In fact, according to the 2022 General Social Survey, fewer than 2 percent of those connected to a mainline church were between the ages of eighteen and thirty-five.[24] Even in churches with active youth groups, youth tend to go on to college or careers, and most do not return to church. Other

---

[23] Barna, "The State of Generosity," accessed November 15, 2025, https://www.barna.com/collections/the-state-of-generosity/.

[24] Ryan Burge, "The Remnant: Inside the World of Young Conservative Christians," Graphs About Religion, August 19, 2024, https://www.graphsaboutreligion.com/p/the-remnant-inside-the-world-of-young.

churches struggle to have enough youth to even form a youth group. As young adults find their way and settle into adult life, few churches are able to build relation*ships* with them or offer relevant ministry opportunities. If young adults show up at church, they often struggle to find other young adults to connect with or activities that appeal to them.

There is a greater phenomenon impacting the church's ability to connect with youth and young adults. In Kevin Wallsten's post titled, "Young People Don't Think Much of American Institutions Anymore" on The Missing Data Depot, he shared this:

> *Very few American high school students currently believe the military, higher education, the media, religious organizations, law enforcement, big business, public schools, or labor unions are serving the country well.*
>
> *It's easy to be dismissive of the attitudes of high school students. But ignoring young people's growing cynicism about our key institutions would be a serious mistake. Nearly every American institution that relies on the voluntary participation of young people now finds itself facing an existential crisis. Colleges and universities, for instance, are on the verge of falling off an "enrollment cliff." Religious organizations are experiencing a "great dechurching." The US military is fighting an unprecedented "recruitment crisis."*[25]

In the podcast *Why Teens Don't Trust the Church,* Kara Powell, author, executive director of the Fuller Youth Institute, and founder of the Tenx10 Collaboration, explains why the youth and young adults are disconnected from churches.

---

[25] Kevin Wallsten, "Young People Don't Think Much of American Christianity," The Missing Data Depot, July 24, 2024, https://themissingdatadepot.substack.com/p/young-people-dont-think-much-of-american.

> *According to some really fascinating research by Springtide (Research Institute), young people (ages) 13 to 25, are three times more likely to have been hurt by organized religion than to trust organized religion. That's pretty stunning data. And we've earned young people's lack of trust, sadly, by our unkindness in the church, by our moral failures, (and) by our hypocrisy.*
>
> *It is hard to keep up with all the moral failures in the church. And so that becomes overwhelming for young people. Another thing that contributes is the hypocrisy—how they see the church and those of us who are Jesus followers saying one thing, but our lives represent something else. So, as a result, they're drifting and not trusting us.*
>
> *When asked what the hard truth is that church leaders don't want to hear about young people in the future, Powell replied, "I think churches are in danger of going the route of Blockbuster (Video). Blockbuster had every advantage in terms of funding, expansion, and scale. But Netflix had creativity and entrepreneurism. (Today) There is one Blockbuster store, whereas Netflix has become dominant because it had an eye to the future."*[26]

Young people are struggling with relational connections. In Ryan Burge's article, "High School Students Are Growing Incredibly Anti-Social,"[27] he states, "There's an empirical reason for my concern—the data about the social lives of high school students is incredibly bleak and honestly makes me very worried for the next generation." In breaking down the data in Monitoring

---

[26] Carey Nieuwhof, "Episode 719: Why Teens Don't Trust the Church: Kara Powell on Why Young Women Are Dropping Out of Church and The Keys to Reaching the Next Generation," Carey Nieuwhof Leadership Podcast, April 1, 2025, https://careynieuwhof.com/episode719/.

[27] Ryan Burge, "High School Students Are Growing Incredibly Anti-Social," Graphs About Religion, April 14, 2025, https://www.graphsaboutreligion.com/p/high-school-students-are-growing.

the Future, 1995-2021, Burge notes this about the share of high school seniors who go on a date once a month or less:

> *In 1995, the vast majority of seniors were going on dates several times a month. In this data, just about one-third of them said that they were going on zero or one date per month. Between 1995 and 2010, the share who dated very little rose to just below 50%. Let's call that an increase of 15 points in about 15 years. From 2010 through 2021, the share who barely went on dates rose to 72%. That's an increase of 22 points in just 11 years. In other words, the rate doubled in recent years.*
>
> *But I know what you are going to say—COVID explains some of it. Yes, I agree with you—there was a noticeable decrease in dating frequency during 2021 and 2022. But in 2010, 48% of 12th graders were dating rarely. In 2019, it was 63%. That's a fifteen-point jump in just nine years. That cannot be explained by a global pandemic. Dating among high school seniors slowed significantly during the 2010s.*[28]

Most young people are searching for connection and community, but many struggle to find a place to connect that feels safe, authentic, and transparent. According to *The State of Religion and Young People 2023,*[29] "Young people are looking for sacred experiences ... they just might not be finding them in places of worship." The report also states a desire for "cultivating a sacred sensibility through connection, relation*ships*, and community." The recommendations from the report for how to help young people encounter the sacred are these: "Relationships. Connection. People. The sacred, for young people, is about

---

[28] Ryan Burge, "High School Students Are Growing Incredibly Anti-Social." Graphs About Religion, April 14, 2025, https://www.graphsaboutreligion.com/p/high-school-students-are-growing.

[29] Springtide Research Institute, *The State of Religion & Young People 2023: Exploring the Sacred* (2023), accessed November 20, 2025, https://springtideresearch.org/research/the-state-of-religion-young-people-2023.

connecting. To build spaces where young people can encounter sacred experiences, leaders need to build spaces where connection thrives—spaces for belonging."

Scott Galloway, an author and professor at New York University's Stern School of Business, warns particularly about the struggles young men face. He shares his concerns in a podcast with Carey Nieuwhof:

> *We're creating a generation of millions of young men who are lonely and not economically or emotionally viable. And, there is nothing more dangerous than a lonely, broke, young man." He adds, "They (young men) start sequestering from society and never really develop skills to be successful professionally. There are 3 million working-age men under the age of 40 who have just given up on working. Half of millennial men aren't dating. They're not even trying because they find it so humiliating and hard.*[30]

Here is the good news. Seventy-eight percent of young people state they are at least slightly spiritual.[31] Researchers are finding that Gen Z reports being less spiritually open as they enter adulthood, yet the majority remain spiritually open. Young adults also appreciate multi-generational opportunities, including mutual mentoring. There is a tremendous opportunity and openness for churches to build relation*ships* with youth and young adults.

However, the approaches of yesteryear will simply not work. Young people desire to be at the table so they can be heard and

---

[30] Carey Nieuwhof, "Episode 646: Prof G (Scott Galloway) on Why a Generation of Young Men are Filled with Rage and Shame," Carey Nieuwhof Leadership Podcast, April 1, 2025, https://careynieuwhof.com/episode646/.

[31] Springtide Research Institute, *The State of Religion & Young People 2023.*

participate. Most of the church's approaches to youth and young adult ministries are not relevant and don't connect well with today's youth and young adults.

And, just to make it even more interesting to connect with the younger generations, Luke Simon offered some fascinating insights in his article titled "The Gen Z Worship War" in Christianity Today. He explains that there seems to be a divide between what female Zoomers (Gen Z) prefer in worship style versus what Zoomer males prefer. The Zoomers who are gravitating towards traditional worship are male, while their female counterparts gravitate more towards worship that includes contemporary Christian music. Simon shares that there are differences in how each views their faith. For example, female Zoomers are more interested in personal authenticity and intimacy with God through personal devotion. For male Zoomers, worship is less about nostalgia and more about nonnegotiables (true faith doesn't blend with the culture). Zoomer men gravitate towards an interest in discipline, self-mastery, and resilience, while female Zoomers resonate with personal connection and devotion to God (themes which appear in contemporary Christian music).[32] These Zoomer observations from Simon indicate it will be difficult for any church to connect with both Zoomer males and Zoomer females.

If churches want to connect with youth and young adults, they must be willing to invest in them. This does not mean merely designating more dollars in the budget or hiring a staff person. It will require investing time, energy, emotion, interest, openness, curiosity, and letting go of programs, ministries, and events that no longer appeal to younger generations.

---

[32] Luke Simon, "The Gen Z Worship War: Men, Women, CCM, Liturgy, Tradition," Christianity Today, May 29, 2025, https://www.christianitytoday.com/2025/05/gen-z-worship-war-men-women-ccm-liturgy-tradition/.

Connecting Relation*ships* and the Impacts of the Nones

Let's first define this unique demographic. The "Nones" is a term used to describe people who are atheists, agnostics, and "nothing in particular." Of the Nones, approximately 20 percent are atheists, 20 percent agnostics, and 60 percent nothing in particular. The total number of Nones has more than quadrupled since 1990. Growing from 5 percent in the 1970s to 7 percent by 1991. Nones now make up about 30 percent, or approximately 80 million, of our American population.

There are now four unique typologies associated with the Nones, as described by Ryan Burge and Tony Jones in their work at The Spiritual Yearning Research Initiative[33] funded by the John Templeton Foundation. The four types are described in The Nones Project, "Who are the Nones, and what do they believe?"[34]

1. **NiNos (None in Name Only):** This group makes up 21% of the Nones. The majority would describe their religious affiliation as nothing in particular. Over half say they pray daily and believe in God without a doubt.

2. **SBRNs (Spiritual but not Religious):** This group makes up 36% of the Nones. They are deeply skeptical of religion but are highly interested in spirituality. Most of this group either never attend church or seldom do. Nine of the ten report that they hardly ever pray. Only 5% say they believe in God without a doubt but are much more likely to believe in a Higher Power. Their spiritual practices may include yoga, meditation, walks in nature, or crystals.

---

[33] John Templeton Fund, Spiritual Yearning Research Initiative, "The Search for Meaning Among the Nonreligious," accessed November 20, 2025, https://www.templeton.org/internal-competiton-fund/the-spiritual-yearning-research-initiative-the-search-for-meaning-among-the-nonreligious.

[34] The Nones Project, "Who are the Nones, and what do they believe," accessed November 20, 2025, https://www.thenonesproject.com/.

3. **Dones:** This group makes up one-third of the Nones. The Dones are literally done with religion in its entirety. Nearly all of the Dones don't pray at all or participate in any religious practices. Interestingly, 77% of the Dones agreed with this statement: "When I die, my existence ends."

4. **Zealous Atheists:** This is the smallest of the Nones at only 11%. The trait that makes this group uniquely different from the others is that about 75% of them have tried to convince someone else to leave religion in the past twelve months. About 17% of this group attend worship once a year or more and pray infrequently.

Regardless of what they are called or how they are defined, there is a significant increase in the number of people with no religious affiliation.

In a Lewis Center for Church Leadership podcast episode titled "Who Are the Nones?" Dr. Ryan Burge explains:

> *The biggest crisis we're facing in America today is a crisis of trust—both institutional and interpersonal trust. Religion used to be really good at showing people that institutions may be bad in some ways, but overall, they do good things because they're made of people. Because churches used to be places of diversity—political diversity, economic diversity, educational diversity—they also taught us that people who are different than us are not bad. But now churches have become homogenized. And that creates silos where you look at other people and say, "You're wrong. We're right. We've got it all figured out over here."*[35]

The issues that drive people away from organized religion are multifaceted. However, you will notice some common themes shared by other reports. The Nones reported these

---

[35] Ryan P. Burge, "Who Are the 'Nones'? An In-Depth Interview with Ryan Burge," Lewis Center for Church Leadership — Leading Ideas, March 1, 2023, https://www.churchleadership.com/leading-ideas/who-are-the-nones-an-in-depth-interview-with-ryan-burge/.

common "key wedge issues" as reasons for being disconnected, according to the American Beliefs Study: Religious Preferences & Practices (December 2023).

Reasons for being disconnected from religion:

- 52% don't trust organized religion
  - 17% somewhat significant factor
  - 69% somewhat, considerably, or very much a factor
- 48% don't trust religious leaders
  - 18% somewhat significant factor
  - 66% somewhat, considerably, or very much a factor
- 48% wasn't relevant to their life
  - 18% somewhat significant factor
  - 66% somewhat, considerably, or very much a factor
- 46% religious people are too judgmental
  - 19% somewhat significant factor
  - 65% somewhat, considerably, or very much a factor
- 42% religion is too focused on money
  - 20% somewhat significant factor
  - 62% somewhat, considerably, or very much a factor
- 41% disillusionment with religion
  - 18% somewhat significant factor
  - 59% somewhat, considerably, or very much a factor
- 40% don't believe in God
  - 16% somewhat significant factor
  - 56% somewhat, considerably, or very much a factor[36]

---

[36] Pew Research Center, "Religious Landscape Study – American Beliefs Study: Religious Preferences & Practices" (December 2023), https://www.pewresearch.org/collections/religious-landscape-study/.

Trust is a huge challenge for institutions in general and, in particular, for the church. This is true at the local, regional, national, and denominational levels. Trust and confidence in institutions have withered, especially in the past few decades. In asking how much confidence people have in organized religion, those saying they had a great deal of trust dropped from 38 percent to 25 percent from 1972 to 1990. In the most recent data, about 15 percent of folks expressed a great deal of confidence in religion, while the share who had hardly any trust has risen from 15 percent in 1972 to 35 percent today.[37]

According to Burge's article "The Nones Have Hit the Ceiling," studies indicate that the increase in the number of Nones has slowed and may have even plateaued. This is true across all generations except the Silent Generation, which saw a 3 percent increase, and the Boomers, which saw a 2 percent increase between 2022 and 2023. The generation with the most significant decrease from 2022 to 2023 was Gen Z (48 percent to 42 percent).[38]

While those 2 to 5 percent year-over-year increases seem to be slowing or stopping, it is still important to understand the percentage of each generation that is considered Nones. This is especially true if building relation*ships* with youth and young adults is desired. Current estimates are that 42 percent of both Millennials and Gen Z are Nones, while only 21 percent of the Silent Generation, 28 percent of the Boomers, and 34 percent of Gen X are Nones. For comparison, the share of Nones among 63-year-olds is about 27 percent. This number represents a thirteen-point jump in twenty birth years versus a five-point

---

[37] Ryan Burge, "Trust and Not Believe? Or Believe and Not Trust?" Graphs About Religion, October 28, 2024, https://www.graphsaboutreligion.com/p/trust-and-not-believe-or-believe.

[38] yan Burge, "The Nones Have Hit a Ceiling," Graphs About Religion, September 16, 2024, https://www.graphsaboutreligion.com/p/the-nones-have-hit-a-ceiling.

jump in the next twenty birth years.[39]

Church leaders often ask what it will take to connect with the Nones. Here is the list from the "2023 American Beliefs Study: Changing Behaviors Within Faith Communities," outlining the top things Nones would like to see in a church or religious community:

- 42% – warm and friendly encounters
- 30% – involvement in social causes
- 27% – social justice advocacy work
- 24% – opportunities for volunteering in the community
- 23% – opportunities to develop personal relation*ships*
- 22% – adult social activities
- 21% – cultural programs (music, drama, art)
- 21% – quality sermons
- 20% – crisis support groups[40]

Looking at the list above, how does your current ministry mix compare to what the Nones would like to see? Which of your ministries are particularly geared towards building new relation*ships* with the Nones within the categories above? What is your church willing to let go of (e.g., ideas, traditions, ineffective ministries, focus, values) to reach the 30 percent of the population known as the Nones?

From the same American Beliefs Study, here is a list of items that only a small percentage of Nones marked as what they would like to see in a church or religious community:

---

[39] Burge, "The Nones Have Hit a Ceiling."

[40] Burge, "The Nones Have Hit a Ceiling."

12% – contemporary worship experiences

11% – online or virtual worship experiences

10% – spiritual discussion groups

9% – traditional worship experiences

9% – singles or college-age groups

8% – marriage enrichment

7% – religious education for children

6% – Bible or scripture study/prayer groups

6% – celebration of sacraments

In reviewing the list above, what percentage of your church's resources (e.g., time, focus, dollars, energy) is invested in these low-interest areas of the Nones? If your church desires to reach the Nones, what shifts would you be willing to make to do so?

In working with churches across the country, we often find it is a struggle to bridge the gap between what the unchurched might be looking for and what the congregation desires, has grown accustomed to, or has become comfortable with. Here are a few areas of the American Beliefs Study[41] featuring key gaps in what Nones and practicing Christians would like to see in a church:

% Practicing Christians		% Nones
89	Quality Sermons	21
85	Warm & Friendly Encounters	42
80	Traditional Worship Services	9
72	Celebration of Sacraments	6

41 Pew Research Center, "Religious Landscape Study."

70	Bible or scripture study/prayer groups	6
64	Family-oriented activities	18

Notice that even the highest-ranking desires for Nones are nowhere close to the percentages of the desires for practicing Christians. For example, 85 percent of practicing Christians scored warm and friendly encounters highly, but even as the top-scoring group, it was still only 42 percent for the Nones. This is a great snapshot of the gaps in values of what's important or relevant for churched people and the Nones. These percentage gaps provide insights into why reaching Nones is so difficult for churches.

Here is the good news. Approximately 80 percent of Americans report being spiritually open. Compare this to approximately 50 percent of the country having no religious affiliation. There is not only great potential, but there is a deep spiritual hunger in our country. To reach the Nones, we will have to invest relationally. It will take time, patience, vulnerability, love, and grace. It will also likely require some shifts in how churches use their time, energy, focus, and resources. To reach this significant portion of our country referred to as the Nones, it will require a whole new movement that includes both clergy and laity—even this is a major shift in how we view the traditional church's roles and responsibilities.

How the Relation*ship* Crisis Impacts the Church

Here is our connection point: trust is built over time through ongoing relation*ships*. Without the presence of the focused demographics highlighted in this chapter in churches, the relation*ships* needed to build that trust are absent. The relational gap widens without an intentional approach to building these relation*ships* outside the church—out in the orbits of the ships we desire to reach.

Building trust is a multifaceted process that involves consistent actions, open communication, and demonstrating reliability. Key elements in building trust include honesty, keeping promises, showing respect, and being vulnerable. Trust is built over time through consistent behavior and is easily broken, so it requires ongoing effort and investment to maintain.

The church's challenge to connect with people relationally has greatly contributed to the resulting impact in the mental health crisis, the disconnect with moms, youth and young adults, and the ability to reach the Nones. The church's relation*ship*-building deficit has certainly led to the decline in local churches, the overall church, and in the unchurched people's perceptions of the church. An intentional focus on going outside the church walls to build new, authentic relation*ships* will need to become central to a church's approach for a vital future.

For the church to once again become the preferred port of call, the congregants will need to voyage into the open seas in their individual relation*ships* and become part of the orbits of the relation*ships,* like those named moms, youth, young adults, Gen Z, the Nones, and those suffering from mental health.

Wrap-Up

> *But how can people call for help if they don't know who to trust? And how can they know who to trust if they haven't heard of the One who can be trusted? And how can they hear if nobody tells them? And how is anyone going to tell them, unless someone is sent to do it? That's*

why Scripture exclaims, A sight to take your breath away! Grand processions of people telling all the good things of God! But not everybody is ready for this, ready to see and hear and act. Isaiah asked what we all ask at one time or another: "Does anyone care, God? Is anyone listening and believing a word of it?" The point is: Before you trust, you have to listen. But unless Christ's Word is preached, there's nothing to listen to.

Romans 10:14 (MSG)

The statistics are overwhelming. The need for the church is great. The desire for spiritual community is very present. Don't get bogged down in the overwhelming statistics and the complex needs identified. We offer this data to help our readers understand the current reality of the world and the tremendous opportunities available for the church to step up and out for such a time as this. The need is now! With the giftedness and passions of your congregation in mind, start with just one of the demographics described in this chapter. What can your port of call (church) offer that could have the greatest impact for the ships (people) in your harbor (neighborhood or mission field)? How can you equip your congregants to feel more confident to intersect with the orbits (e.g., activities, hobbies, organizational affiliations) of the ships you feel called to reach? In the coming chapters, we will guide you with some options, templates, and resources to help you narrow your focus to a manageable next step.

Now that we have firmly established why a shift in the church's focus must be rooted in relation*ships,* let's dive into how. Let's continue the journey together.

Key Points

1. While the world is indeed deeply divided, there is a

growing desire for connection and spirituality.

2. A healthy, vital church (preferred port of call) is exactly what our culture needs. However, the church will need to rethink how it connects within its context in more relevant and relatable ways.

3. At its core, the church is based on building healthy relation*ships* (with one another and with Jesus). In our postmodern, post-Christian culture, the church must refocus its attention, equipping, and resources on building new relation*ships* beyond the harbor and into the open seas.

4. Mothers are looking for a sense of community, support, a seat and a voice at leader*ship* tables, and resources for parenting and well-being, but often find that the church does not fulfill or recognize these needs.

5. Youth and young adults are spiritually open, but the majority of churches are disconnected in their approach and in their relevant ministries to reach this growing, increasingly unchurched population.

6. Mental health is a crisis the church needs to address and be a part of finding and participating in a pathway to improved mental health. At its core, the church can have a profoundly positive impact on mental health if it understands and embraces the fact that 80 percent of mental health treatment comes from belonging to a loving, supportive community.

7. The Nones are a substantial part of our American demographics. In addition, a great majority of the Nones are spiritually open. However, to reach this demographic, the church must rethink its approach to building spiritual community with them. What the church has been doing is, by and large, not working, as

evidenced by the typical shrinking church size and its older, homogenous congregations.

8. We are called as Christians to love our neighbors. Yet the church has become insular, inwardly focused, and disconnected from the neighborhoods it is called to reach. To fully live out our lives as disciples of Jesus, we must regain our focus on loving our neighbors above saving our churches.

Case Study

The COVID pandemic changed everything—absolutely everything. Remote work and remote learning became the new norm. Grocery and meal delivery spiked. Zoom became the major lifeline to the outside world. Viewership of streaming services surged as more people sought home entertainment. Some even received auto insurance rebates from insurance companies due to the dramatic decrease in claims because people were driving considerably less.

People hunkered down and cocooned with their family or "COVID bubble." This was an unprecedented time. People were fearful, and anxiety was high. No one knew what the future held. There were conflicting views, opinions, and recommendations (even amongst professionals and experts) on important topics such as gathering, vaccinating, and masking. This mixed messaging and the personal or regional values that decisions were based on only caused more fear, anger, anxiety, and division. Needless to say, it was a difficult time to be a leader navigating people, organizations, and companies through such unprecedented situations.

One particular church in southwest Missouri took a very intentional approach during the initial stages of COVID. The church was less than six years old. The growing congregation was multi-generational but leaned towards the Millennial generation with young families. Together, the highly relational pastor and the missionally aligned leader*ship* board made a very important decision. They knew their young church didn't have the long-term relation*ships* to anchor themselves to one another that older churches did. They also understood that their congregation of Millennials and Silent Generation members was struggling in their own unique ways. To support and care for their congregation, these leaders divided the church roster and made personal phone calls to every congregant. This was not a one-time call, but their intentional and authentic approach was repeated multiple times until the congregation began to gather again.

Knowing the need to stay connected with the children, this church took another innovative approach. A variety of congregants, some with children and some without, videotaped a children's interactive message each week. The unique approach was fresh and precious. Some even reported that they didn't want the videos to stop, even when the church could safely gather again!

While some churches never fully reconvened their congregations post-COVID, this church not only came back strongly, but it has surpassed its pre-COVID levels and is a thriving, vital congregation. The wise leaders of this church realized that relation*ships* matter. Caring for people matters. Reaching out and letting people know they are loved matters. Reaching out and praying with people matters. Reaching out to see what people need and doing everything you can to meet that need matters. Yes, those phone calls required an investment of time and energy from the leaders who were also managing their own pandemic uncertainties. But their actions held the congregation together by investing in relation*ships*.

The congregants of this church were no different from those in other churches navigating the same pandemic waters. But the difference in this church is that the leaders demonstrated authentic, relational servant leader*ship!*

CHAPTER 2

Our Disconnected Orbits

The thief's purpose is to steal and kill and destroy. My purpose is to give them a rich and satisfying life.

John 10:10 (NLT)

We were created to thrive—not just survive, but to live fully, deeply, and fruitfully. God wants this for us individually, but God also intends for us to thrive in relation*ship* with one another. God created us to live in community—a fleet of (relation)*ships.*

From the very beginning, God revealed Himself as Father, Son, and Holy Spirit—three distinct Persons, yet one God. This mysterious relation*ship* within the Trinity is our model of community. God has always existed in a loving, mutual *relationship* within the Trinity. The very first chapter of the Bible introduces this Triune God, saying, "Let us [plural] make mankind in our image, in our likeness" (Genesis 1:26, NIV). So, when God created us in God's image, God created us for relation*ships* too.

God reiterates this in Genesis 2:18, musing, "It is not good for the man to be alone" (NIV). The Creator said this before sin had even entered the world. Relation*ship* with others is not just something that would be nice; it is necessary.

Jesus prayed in his High Priestly prayer in John 17:21, "That all of them may be one, Father, just as you are in me and I am in you" (NIV). One of the last things Jesus prayed before his death was that we would experience unity and relation*ship* just like he does with the Father and the Holy Spirit.

We are made for connection. And yet, as we discussed in Chapter 1, we saw the erosion of that connection, both for individuals and for the church. Ryan Burge, in his article "Dropping out of Everything," says:

> *Instead of being shaped by in-person interactions at the town council meeting, the local Catholic Church, or the halls of the local community college or university, they (the "dropouts") are holed up in their rooms, letting algorithms feed them more of what they think they want to see.*[42]

Many factors have contributed to our current relational and societal disconnection: reliance on digital relation*ships,* mental health challenges, a high value on individualism, and work that consumes our lives. The COVID pandemic further accelerated the erosion of our social skills during months and even years of isolation.

In the April 2023 *Time* magazine article "We Have Put Individualism Ahead of the Common Good for Too Long," Richard Weissbourd and Chris Murphy noted America's tension between individualism and collectivism, contending:

> *America's genius lies not just in our spirit of entrepreneur***ship** *and pick-yourself-up-by-your-bootstraps individualism, but also in our decision to make sure that this value on personal responsibility and success is never absolute. To varying degrees over the course of our history, it has been matched by a concern for the community and the collective. We measured success both by how well we were doing and how well the communities and the*

[42] Ryan Burge, "Dropping Out of Everything," Graphs About Religion, April 22, 2024, https://www.graphsaboutreligion.com/p/dropping-out-of-everything.

> *country we belonged to were doing, and we tended to view our individual and collective well-being as powerfully entwined.*[43]

Weissbourd and Murphy view the culprits to be declines in religious participation and social outings and clubs, fueled in part by television, which keeps us at home. Workplaces also became more focused on profit than on employee well-being and solidarity, and we started lionizing those who stepped over others to get ahead. While those people have always existed in society, they were usually identified and treated as outliers who needed to be constrained, not as examples of American greatness.

Relying on others is not highly valued in our current culture. Like toddlers, we announce defiantly, "I can do it myself!" We can find out how to do just about anything on YouTube. We opt to buy a new tool from Facebook Marketplace before asking a neighbor if we can borrow theirs. We'll Google for an answer rather than reach out to a human being. We find our answers online, all alone, by ourselves.

Many of us live quiet little lives in our private homes, where we back out of our garage in the morning, maybe wave at the neighbor walking their dog, and drive to work. We work at our jobs all day, then get back in our car, drive home, pull into our garage, and close the door behind us without ever having to interact with anyone in our neighborhood. Our life's orbits don't intersect with anyone else's life orbits.

Or—better yet—we can now work from home. We don't even need to cross paths with the dog-walking neighbor whose name we don't know anyway. We don't even need to wear pants! We cry triumphantly, "I don't need anyone."

---

[43] Chris Murphy and Richard Weissbourd, "We Have Put Individualism Ahead of the Common Good for Too Long," *TIME*, April 11, 2023, https://time.com/6269091/individualism-ahead-of-the-common-good-for-too-long/.

This is not necessarily a new sentiment. Kenny Rogers sang in 1981 that "we don't need each other," then questioned, "or do we?"[44]

Perhaps isolation and individualism have always been a challenge, as John Donne, English poet and cleric, claimed in his 1624 poem *No Man Is an Island:*

No man is an island,
Entire of itself;
Every man is a piece of the continent,
A part of the main.

If a clod be washed away by the sea,
Europe is the less,
As well as if a promontory were:
As well as if a manor of thy friend's
Or of thine own were.

Any man's death diminishes me,
Because I am involved in mankind.
And therefore never send to know for whom the bell tolls;
It tolls for thee.[45]

Jesus knew the importance of being connected with others—to have interlinked and overlapping orbits in our relation*ships.* He saw the isolation of lepers who had lived their lives crying "Unclean!" to anyone who came near. He gravitated toward the people that religious and civic communities ostracized as sinners. Rather than fleeing from the demon-possessed, Jesus drew near.

The disciples and early followers of the Way emulated Jesus' example and even expounded on it: "Every day they continued

---

[44] Kenny Rogers, "Through the Years," on Share Your Love, Liberty Records, 1981.

[45] John Donne, Meditation XVII from *Devotions upon Emergent Occasions* (1624), quoted in "No Man Is an Island," *AllPoetry,* accessed November 15, 2025, https://allpoetry.com/No-man-is-an-island.

to meet together in the temple courts. They broke bread in their homes and ate together with glad and sincere hearts" (Acts 2:46, NIV). Not only did they understand the importance of being connected, but the result was a growth in their movement.

So, how does the church address the pervasive disconnection that has eroded our society in recent years?

The Disconnect of a Sunday-Centric Model

Pastors were told in previous years, "Everything points to Sunday." A youth program's goal: get them in the seats on Sunday. Outreach activity goal: get them in the seats on Sunday. "Invite a Friend to Church" Sunday, the attractional church model, Sunday school contests, VBS—all had the ultimate goal of filling our churches and the offering plate on Sunday.

Or, maybe they will come on Sunday if we put a catchy phrase on the church marquee, such as:

- "Need a lifeguard? Ours walks on water."
- "Honk if you love Jesus. Text while driving if you want to meet Him."
- "Prayer: the original wireless connection."
- "Come in – our church is prayer-conditioned."
- "Join us Sunday – faith, hope, and free coffee."

We hoped that people would come in and check us out. It is unlikely that those clever messages actually led a new guest to attend worship. But was getting people to fill the pews on Sunday really the goal of the gospel? Jesus didn't come to start a weekly event; he came to initiate a Kingdom—to create a movement. That means transformed lives, ongoing disciple*ship*, and a people who follow him in every part of life, not just an hour or two on Sundays. Jesus modeled a way of life intended for all 168 hours of the week, not just one.

Many churches today (especially in the Western world) unintentionally equate spiritual success with how many people show up on Sunday. Big buildings, packed pews, and slick services became signs of health. But biblically, Jesus wasn't trying to build a crowd. He was raising up a Kingdom of disciples, specifically "sent" disciples—not a Kingdom of "spectator" disciples.

Crowds followed Jesus for miracles and free food, but when he called for self-denial and sacrifice, most left. He didn't chase them. He focused on depth with the few (like the Twelve), not shallow engagement with the many.

So here's the disconnection:

Many Western Churches' Focus	**Jesus' Missional Priority was**
Sunday attendance	Daily obedience (Luke 9:23)
Programs and events	Personal transformation (Ephesians 4:22-24)
Entertaining messages by celebrity pastors	Challenging truth (John 6:60-66)
Keeping people comfortable and happy	Calling people to carry the cross (Matthew 16:34)
Measuring success by numbers	Measuring Kingdom impact by disciple-making (Matthew 28:19-20)

The reality is that spending an hour or two on a Sunday morning—although a beautiful time to gather to worship—does not resolve the disconnection afflicting so many inside and outside the church. A regular Sunday attender can still be isolated, anonymous, unknown, and stagnant in their faith. In fact, in our on-the-ground experience, we have encountered too many "religious people" who have attended worship services for years but would not be described as mature or even maturing disciples. Their attendance became more about habit and a sense of obligation rather than growing, behaving, and acting more Christlike.

His purpose was to equip God's people
for the work of serving and building up the body of Christ
until we all reach the unity of faith and knowledge of God's Son.
God's goal is for us to become mature adults—to be fully grown,
measured by the standard of the fullness of Christ.

Ephesians 4:12-13 (CEB)

The Disconnect of AI Companionship

Most people long for community in some form. Humans are wired for connection and relation*ships.* This desire goes way back to humans being made in the image of a Triune God who is community. People crave a sense of belonging, being seen, and being valued.

Even those who enjoy solitude often still want and need meaningful connection. They may just desire the connection in smaller doses or more intentional ways. They search in a variety of places:

- Online
- Meetup apps
- Work
- Hobby and interest groups (e.g., art classes, book clubs, sports teams)

- Service clubs
- Volunteering
- Alcoholics Anonymous, Narcotics Anonymous, or Al-Anon
- Maybe church
- Spiritual communities that mainline Christians wouldn't identify as "church"

Some people are even exploring virtual relation*ships* with AI-powered companions. AI companionship is rapidly gaining traction, especially among young people, driven by the increasing sophistication of AI technology and the desire for emotional support and connection in a world grappling with social isolation. According to a report from Global Market Insights,[46] this $14 billion-plus global app market is used by people across all generations. However, there is rapid growth in usage within the Gen Z and Millennial generations. About 28 percent of men aged eighteen to thirty-four have tried an AI girlfriend app. Seventy-two percent of U.S. teens use AI companion apps.

These AI chatbots or virtual assistants simulate human-like conversations and provide companionship, emotional support, and platonic and even romantic relation*ships*. AI companions can even offer medication reminders for seniors suffering from memory loss. AI companions may seem like a reasonable solution to the isolation and loneliness epidemic. An AI companion can, indeed, provide emotional support and personalized conversations, as well as be constantly available. An AI companion will not offer criticism, judgment, or hypocrisy.

---

[46] Global Market Insights, "AI Companion App Market," May 2025, https://www.gminsights.com/industry-analysis/ai-companion-app-market.

However, the dangers can outweigh the benefits. Let's explore some of the concerns and dangers associated with this growing trend:

Emotional Dependence and Isolation

Overreliance on a nonhuman AI companion can lead to emotional dependence, in which individuals begin to prefer their AI relation*ships* over real-world interactions. After all, these companions are designed to be highly responsive, available at all times, and offer personalized and predictable responses. They don't argue, ignore, or challenge.

For someone who may already be struggling with healthy social skills and emotional intelligence, this false sense of intimacy and emotional support could discourage users from connecting and building genuine relation*ships* with people in the real world. This can create further feelings of isolation and alienation, especially if people start to avoid face-to-face social interactions. True relation*ships* are complex and messy when compared to the simplicity of AI interactions.

Unrealistic Expectations

AI companions are designed to please users, offering emotional support, attention, validation, and sometimes even affection. However, these interactions are artificial and tailored to the user's desires. When these same responses from real-life relation*ships* are not realized, it could further erode genuine human relation*ships*.

Real-life relation*ships* require compromise, communication, and effort. The idealized nature of AI companions—who can be programmed to respond perfectly—might set expectations that are unattainable in human relation*ships*, leading to frustration or dissatisfaction in the real world. In fact, new research reveals that 72 percent of teens have used AI companions (chatbots), and an astonishing 31 percent of them prefer AI to human companionship.[47]

Lack of Genuine Emotional Reciprocity

A conversation with an AI companion is simulated. Artificial companions have no capacity for true emotional understanding or for reciprocating emotions. True emotional intimacy involves mutual understanding, empathy, and vulnerability, which AI cannot genuinely provide. This can leave people feeling emotionally unfulfilled in the long term.

Mental Health Implications

Ironically, people struggling with mental health issues due to disconnection and isolation could experience exacerbation of their existing depression, anxiety, or loneliness. The expected "cure" becomes more of a hindrance. AI companions might provide temporary relief, but they do not offer the deep psychological support that human relation*ships* or professional therapy can. They can't diagnose or treat mental health disorders. Their inability to offer real therapeutic support could make underlying mental health issues worse or cause users to avoid seeking professional help.

Impact on Relation*ship* Skills

In a September 2023 article, the National Library of Medicine reported: "With limited social interactions, disrupted routines, and imposed lockdowns during the pandemic, children encountered unusual early social, cognitive, and emotional development challenges. These factors, combined with the stress

---

[47] Jen Christensen, "Teens Are Turning to AI Companions for Wellness—Often More Than to People," CNN, July 16, 2025, https://www.cnn.com/2025/07/16/health/teens-ai-companion-wellness.

experienced by parents and the caregivers, dismantled a never-ending list of obstacles for young children's ability to develop social-emotional skills."[48]

Similar to the stunted relation*ship* skills for children during the pandemic, building relation*ships* with AI can hinder a person's ability to develop key interactions with others, such as conflict resolution, empathy, communication, and vulnerability.

Since AI companions are designed to simulate positive interactions without the complexities of real human emotions, they cannot challenge users or encourage personal growth in the same way human relation*ships* can. Healthy interpersonal engagement allows the opportunity to learn how to handle real-life relation*ship* dynamics such as disagreements, negotiation, and emotional support. When this is lacking, people may struggle to adapt to the unpredictability and nuance of human relation*ships*, especially in situations that require compromise and emotional labor.

Theological and Ethical Issues

God made HUMANS in God's image. This is what sets us apart from the rest of creation. Jesus' response to the question of "Which is the greatest commandment in the law?" is "Love the Lord your God with all your heart and with all your soul and with all your mind." This is the first and greatest commandment. And the second is like it: "Love your neighbor as yourself" (Matthew 22: 37-39, NIV). Choosing an AI companion over my neighbor not only poses the risks noted above but, most importantly, likely opposes everything Jesus came to teach about how to live and love.

---

[48] Michelle Rodriguez-Monge, Isabela Iglesias-Peña, and Francesco Chiappelli, "CoViD-19 Effects on Social-Emotional Development: Impact of Early Intervention," *Bioinformation 19,* no. 9, September 30, 2023, https://pmc.ncbi.nlm.nih.gov/articles/PMC10625367/#s4.

The dehumanized, programmed responses to cater to the user's every desire are in direct conflict with these scriptural teachings and the way of life taught by Jesus: "Be kind and compassionate to one another, forgiving each other, just as in Christ God forgave you" (Ephesians 4:32, NIV). The imitation of Christ's humility in "Do nothing out of selfish ambition or vain conceit. Rather, in humility value others above yourselves, not looking to your own interests but each of you to the interests of the others" (Philippians 2:3-4, NIV). The principle of the Golden Rule tells us, "So in everything, do to others what you would have them do to you, for this sums up the Law and the Prophets" (Matthew 7:12, NIV).

The Church Connection

Churches are not usually early adopters of anything new or cutting-edge. This is especially true when it comes to technology. While large and mega-sized churches are more likely to be early adopters, the average U.S. church does not typically have or is unwilling to allocate dollars for technology. Other times, churches struggle to find people with the knowledge and skills to resource and install the hardware and software needed or the personnel to run and maintain the technology. Yet another issue that creates stumbling blocks to the adoption of technology is foundational values and disagreements over whether technology should be used in the church. For these reasons and more, churches are typically late adopters at best and likely a decade or two behind current cultural technology trends—and the use of AI is no exception.

Not being aware of current technology trends and how they affect your neighbors and your community perpetuates a disconnection that the church is already struggling with. For church leaders to bury their heads in the sand and ignore the impact technology has on those in their mission field is a demonstration of cultural incompetence and often even emotional incompetence (more on those topics in Chapter 3). For church leaders to turn a blind eye to the growing concerns about how AI is affecting relation*ships* and fail to address them is not loving and caring for our neighbors. For church leaders to ignore the AI companion trends and fail to help the congregation and the greater community become more aware of these trends, their ethical and unethical uses, and their dangers is being unfaithful to their role in forming and instructing disciples. The church needs to be part of finding a healthy way forward to utilize the benefits and values of technology without allowing the risks and dangers to destroy humankind.

The Disconnect Related to the Mental Health Crisis

There are multiple ways that the church has become disconnected from the topics surrounding mental health and those suffering from mental illness. As described in Chapter 1 by the Surgeon General, 80 percent of the treatment for mental health happens in communities that are connected, that are supportive of women and minorities, have childcare, and have good educational and employment opportunities. We are not suggesting that the church is the answer for the mental health crisis or that it can offer everything the Surgeon General suggested. However, the church has a growing relational disconnection with moms and young adults—some of the same demographics who have higher percentages of suffering from mental illness. In addition, where the church once helped its communities address issues, concerns, and gaps, it has grown increasingly insular, self-focused on its survival, and judgmental of the changing culture. The church has yet to realize, understand, and admit its share of the responsibility for the culture's disconnection in relation*ships*, which has led to so much of the suffering in the world.

In Chapter 1, we provided statistics and information about the mental health crisis plaguing the modern world. We will now dive into one of the most prevalent mental health struggles— isolation—the church's related disconnection, and some possible new ways forward to regain the connection, relation*ships*, and the resulting impact.

Isolation

False machine-generated relations, social media, and COVID have combined to make a toxic reality of isolation.

Isolation can have a significant impact on mental health, affecting both emotional and cognitive well-being. It can increase feelings of loneliness. Being "alone" is different from isolation. Prolonged isolation can lead to deep feelings of loneliness. Humans are social creatures, and a lack of interaction with others can create a sense of disconnection and sadness. Loneliness has been linked to a higher risk of depression and anxiety, as individuals may begin to feel that they are unimportant, unloved, or forgotten.

Such isolation can lead to a higher risk of depression and anxiety, amplifying negative thoughts and feelings. Without regular social support, it becomes harder to manage stress and cope with emotions, leading to an increased risk of depression and anxiety. Being alone for extended periods can also result in rumination, in which a person repeatedly replays negative thoughts or worries in their mind.

Isolation can lower self-esteem and feelings of self-worth. Without validation from others, some may start to doubt their own value or worth, feeling as if they are invisible or unworthy of connection: Do people even know I exist? Do they even care IF I exist? Over time, this can erode self-esteem and self-confidence, making it harder to engage with others or form healthy relation*ships* in the future.

Isolation may weaken previous coping mechanisms. With reduced access to social support systems that people typically rely on during difficult times, coping mechanisms such as talking through problems, seeking advice and prayer, or engaging in shared activities are compromised. One's name on a prayer list in the Sunday bulletin does not suffice. As a result, individuals may turn to unhealthy coping strategies like substance abuse, overeating, or withdrawal.

Isolation often even impacts a person's physical health, which in turn can affect mental well-being. Chronic stress and lack of physical activity due to isolation can increase the risk of conditions such as heart disease, hypertension, and sleep disturbances.[49]

Social skills decline in the midst of isolation. People may lose confidence in their abilities to interact with others. This can lead to a cycle in which the fear of social interaction or difficulty engaging with others makes it even harder to break free from isolation.

The isolation of grandparents confined to nursing homes, young stay-at-home moms, and those suffering from chronic illness, preventing them from leaving their homes, cannot be assuaged by a Sunday-centric response to a faith community, even when broadcast through live-streaming. Here is one example of the church's disconnection from the isolation epidemic. With the declining financial resources of churches, the pastor or staff member who was once paid to provide visitation

---

49 Julianne Holt-Lunstad, Timothy B. Smith, and Mark Baker, "Loneliness, Isolation, andCardiovascular Health," *Heart 102*, no. 9, 2015, accessed November 15, 2025, https://pmc.ncbi.nlm.nih.gov/articles/PMC5831910/.

or pastoral care is no longer able to do so. Unfortunately, these responsibilities are too often not taken up by the church's disciples to care for their fellow congregants. In addition, churches have failed to transition to a healthier culture of congregational care, instead relying on a pastoral care model. A congregational care approach is not only more sustainable but also biblical—it is part of a disciple's responsibility and privilege.

John Wesley emphasized that disciple*ship* is inherently social and involves actively caring for one another, a concept he termed "social holiness." He believed that genuine Christian faith is expressed through loving relation*ships* and mutual support within a community, where believers encourage, challenge, and help each other grow in faith. This social aspect of disciple*ship* includes practicing works of mercy, such as providing for the needs of the less fortunate and advocating for justice, as well as holding each other accountable in our spiritual growth. Doesn't this sound just like the community the Surgeon General said is needed for mental health improvement?

> *Dear friends, do you think you'll get anywhere in this*
> *if you learn all the right words but never do anything?*
> *Does merely talking about faith indicate that a person really has it?*
> *For instance, you come upon an old friend dressed in rags and half-starved and say,*
> *"Good morning, friend! Be clothed in Christ! Be filled with the Holy Spirit!"*
> *and walk off without providing so much as a coat or a cup of soup—where does that get you? Isn't it obvious that God-talk without God-acts is outrageous nonsense?*
>
> **James 2:14-17 (MSG)**

People's Basic Needs for Belonging, Purpose, and Impact

To combat this isolation and disconnect, the church can play a significant role in meeting people's basic needs for belonging, purpose, and impact by focusing on creating a supportive community, offering meaningful roles within that community, and fostering opportunities for individuals to contribute to both the church and their community.

For people to have their complete needs met, the basic, physiological, and emotional requirements for well-being must all be present. Take a look at this diagram outlining the various levels of human need according to Maslow's Hierarchy of Needs:

From the bottom of the hierarchy upwards, the needs are as follows: physiological (e.g., food and clothing), safety and security (e.g., health and employment), love and belonging (e.g., friend*ships* and family), self-esteem (e.g., confidence and achievement), and self-actualization (e.g., acceptance and purpose). Physiological and safety needs are considered basic needs. Esteem, belonging, and love are considered psychological needs. At the top of the pyramid, you will find the self-fulfillment need of self-actualization. Needs lower down in the hierarchy must be satisfied before individuals can attend to the needs higher up in the pyramid.[50]

Knowing the importance of meeting people's basic needs, Jesus taught us to feed the hungry, clothe the naked, care for the widows, focus on the least of these, heal the sick, and provide water for the thirsty. Yet, it was not intended for us to stop at solely meeting people's basic needs. Jesus also told us to love our neighbors as ourselves. He knew we would struggle to move past those basic needs into building new relation*ships* and helping people feel a sense of belonging and purpose, so he gave us the Great Commandment to "love your neighbor as yourself" to remind us and set these expectations.

A healthy, effective church pays attention to its people's overall, or holistic, well-being. This includes people already connected to the life of the church as well as people in the community. The church is missing the boat if it pays attention only to people's spiritual health. If a person's basic needs are not first being met, it is difficult (if not impossible) to help them grow and have their psychological and spiritual needs met.

Too frequently, churches engage in lovely "outreach" efforts such as collecting canned goods for the local food pantry,

---

[50] Saul McLeod, "Maslow's Hierarchy of Needs," *Simply Psychology*, last modified April 1, 2024, https://www.simplypsychology.org/maslow.html.

gathering socks or mittens for children at the local school, or assembling holiday baskets for homebound neighbors. These acts of generosity and kindness are a great start. Yet they are just that—a start, not the endgame that Jesus had in mind. How are friendships being built? How is the church providing some of those higher needs?

Reflect on some of the disconnection points identified in this chapter. Can you identify the connection to the human need for each? What insights does this bring forward for you as a Christ-follower? Your church? Who does your church intentionally and routinely connect with now? Who in your church has struggled to connect? Who are the disconnected in your community, and how are you individually and as a congregation bridging this connection gap?

Belonging: Creating an All-Embracing Community

The church can create an atmosphere where everyone feels welcome and accepted, regardless of their background or current life circumstances. A tried-and-true model has been small groups that allow people to build relation*ships* in a safe, loving environment. These small groups can be formed based on shared interests or topics—something we will explore in a later chapter.

Emphasizing the importance of diversity within the church community can help foster a deeper sense of belonging for people from different walks of life. When a person attends a church, do they see faces that resemble their own? What does the church leader*ship* look like? Is there accommodation for those who don't speak the dominant language? Is there diversity in the genres and styles of music? Is the diversity in offerings limited to only language translation?

Churches are some of the most segregated groups in

the U.S.—especially on Sunday mornings. But a healthy intercultural congregation might well be the only place where lives could intersect in a truly diverse way. Children with single adults, black with white, affluent with homeless, teens with octogenarians. Learning, loving, and growing together. Regular social events, potlucks, family nights, or special gatherings can create opportunities for people to interact and develop friendships, fostering a sense of belonging beyond just attending services. However, to truly build relation*ships* across the divides, most churches will need to be more intentional about inviting and shifting their activities and approaches to be more relevant and focused on relation*ship*-building.

Someone seeking a sense of belonging may ask—whether consciously or unconsciously—questions such as: "Do I attend or do I belong? What input might I have here? Am I just someone who receives, or can I contribute? Will my voice be heard? Do I know and understand the 'secret language' others use?" A new attender to a church will instantly know they do not belong when a Sunday school teacher dismisses the class and says, "Okay, everyone, you know the drill." Or the announcements include, "This week, we're having all our usual church activities."

Purpose: Encouraging Service and Ministry Participation

One of the most powerful ways to help people find purpose is by inviting them to serve. Typically, a church offers opportunities to serve—whether through ministry teams (e.g., children's ministry, music ministry, outreach), volunteering for local outreach programs, or assisting with the church's administrative needs. However, this leaves out a crucial aspect of what a "newcomer" has to offer. What would it look like if we created an atmosphere that asks, "Tell me about your passions and your skills. What were you seeking when you decided to attend the church? Where do you see a gap that you might like to fill? What and how would you like to contribute to the life of the church?" Perhaps an entirely new way of serving will surface simply because a church asks someone to identify, name, and use their God-given gifts.

The church can also help people discover their unique spiritual gifts and talents through workshops, classes, or personal counseling, guiding them to serve in areas that align with their gifts, abilities, and passions.

Impact: Longing to Know that our Lives Matter

We all want to make an impact in the world. That's why the genealogies in the Bible were so important. This is highlighted in the second chapter of Ezra, where a group of Israelites returns from exile but cannot verify their priestly descent. As a result, they were excluded from serving as priests, pending a decision from God. The proof of their genealogy was crucial for their roles and identity in post-exilic Israel. In addition, this situation also highlights the tension between heritage and inclusion.

The yearning to make an impact and positively (or even negatively) influence others has blossomed into a viable profession since the early 2010s. CNBC posted in September 2024 that 57 percent of Gen Zers wanted to become influencers.[51] Today, even the youngest in our society know the importance of their influence on others. One youngster, when asked how she felt about moving to a new school next year, responded, "I'm just glad I was able to make an impact these past two years." She's ten years old!

---

[51] Gili Malinsky, "57% of Gen Zers Want to Be Influencers—but 'It's Constant, Monday Through Sunday,' Says Creator," *CNBC Make It*, September 14, 2024, https://www.cnbc.com/2024/09/14/more-than-half-of-gen-z-want-to-be-influencers-but-its-constant.html.

The church has an opportunity to align with this trend by empowering individuals to make a tangible difference in their communities and the world. This can include mission trips, food drives, shelter work, or advocacy for justice. Faith communities can work alongside local organizations that serve vulnerable populations (the homeless, refugees, prisoners, etc.), allowing members to participate in impactful work and see the difference they are making in people's lives. The church can inspire members to pursue lives that leave a lasting impact on society.

The Five Pillars and Dimensions of Well-Being

Psychologist Martin Seligman proposed five pillars of well-being in his PERMA model. PERMA stands for Positive Emotions, Engagement, Relation*ships*, Meaning, and Accomplishment. He asserted that these five components of a fulfilled life provide the first indications of a prosperous life.[52] You will notice how these five pillars align very closely to Maslow's Hierarchy of Needs covered earlier in this chapter.

Jesus may have a different slant on what it means to thrive. His teachings and life give us a clear picture of what a whole, flourishing human life looks like in the Kingdom of God. Based on Jesus' words and actions—particularly in places like the Greatest Commandment (Matthew 22:37-39), the Sermon on the Mount (Matthew 5–7), and his relational model of disciple*ship*—we can reasonably identify five core dimensions that align with how Jesus defines human thriving:

Spiritual Vitality - Relation*ship* with God

"Love the Lord your God with all your heart, soul, and mind."

Matthew 22:37, NIV

---

[52] Marcus Raitner, "The Five Pillars of Well-Being," Marcus Raitner, June 26, 2020, https://raitner.de/en/2020/06/the-five-pillars-of-well-being/.

Thriving begins with being deeply rooted in God—abiding in God, trusting God's Word, and living from a place of worship, prayer, and dependence on the Spirit.

Relational Health - Loving others well

"Love your neighbor as yourself."

Matthew 22:39, NIV

Jesus taught that love for others is inseparable from love for God. Forgiveness, peacemaking, compassion, and community are all vital signs of a flourishing life.

Emotional Wholeness - Internal peace and integrity

"Blessed are the pure in heart ... the peacemakers ... those who mourn."

Matthew 5:3-10, NIV

Jesus acknowledged our emotional lives and invited people to bring their brokenness into the light. He healed hearts, not just bodies. Thriving includes dealing honestly with fear, grief, and joy.

Purposeful Calling - Living with Kingdom purpose

"Seek first the Kingdom of God."

Matthew 6:33, ESV

Jesus calls his followers to a life of mission, justice, and stewardship. Thriving means knowing your God-given gifts and using them in ways that reflect the Kingdom and bless others.

Physical and Material Stewardship - Embodied faith

"Give us this day our daily bread" (Matthew 6:11, NRSV).

Jesus met physical needs and taught his followers to care for the poor, rest, and not worry about possessions. A thriving life includes caring for the body (not limited to the church) and using resources wisely.

These five dimensions—spiritual, relational, emotional, purposeful, and physical—are interconnected, not isolated from one another. Jesus' vision of thriving is holistic, deeply rooted in the love of God, and expressed through everyday life.

How can this be fostered in a relationally healthy church? This is what the church is all about—family, the Body of Christ.

A thriving church isn't measured by attendance but by the depth of transformation in its people. When church leaders intentionally nurture the five core dimensions of human thriving exemplified by Christ—spiritual vitality, relational health, emotional wholeness, purposeful calling, and physical/material stewardship—they are not just meeting individual needs. They're forming whole disciples equipped to bring healing, hope, and renewal to the world around them. The fullness of the Body of Christ is exemplified when there is human transformation and thriving both inside *and outside* the church's congregation and walls.

When people learn to abide in Christ daily—not just believe in him—they begin to experience peace, conviction, and guidance that shapes everything else. Abiding in Christ means maintaining a close, vital, and continuous relation*ship* with Jesus, relying on him as the source of life and strength, and allowing his teachings and love to shape one's thoughts, actions, and character. It's a dynamic process of remaining connected to Christ, much like a branch remains connected to the vine, drawing life and fruitfulness from it (John 15). A church that emphasizes spiritual practices (prayer, scripture, worship, dependence on the Spirit) creates a foundation for resilient faith.

Thriving disciples are not isolated; they are formed in relation*ships*. Small groups, mentoring, conflict resolution, and shared life matter deeply. When churches foster authentic, grace-filled relation*ships,* people begin to embody the love of Christ beyond church walls.

Disciple*ship* is stunted when people are emotionally fragmented. Jesus met people in their pain, doubt, fear, and grief—and so must we. Equipping leaders and volunteers to be emotionally present and spiritually grounded creates space for real healing and deep maturity.

When people discover that their work, talents, and life circumstances are part of God's mission, they stop seeing church as a Sunday event and start living as ambassadors of the Kingdom. The church must help people discern and activate their unique callings in their neighborhoods, schools, and workplaces (see *Marketplace Multipliers*[53] for more information about this movement).

Jesus healed bodies and fed the hungry. The church thrives when it cares for the whole person. Teaching stewardship, encouraging rest, supporting those in financial distress, and promoting justice aren't side projects—they're central to disciple-making.

The result is healthy disciples who transform communities. When a church focuses on helping people thrive where they are, disciple*ship* becomes deeply personal and powerfully missional.

---

[53] Wayne Schmidt, Carrie Whitcher, and Kay Kotan, *Expanding the Reach Through Marketplace Multipliers* (Market Square Books, 2021), https://kaykotan.com/marketplacemultiplier-home.

Thriving people don't just consume—they contribute. They become the hands and feet of Jesus in their cities, workplaces, and homes. They don't just attend church—they become the Church, planting seeds of renewal wherever they go.

Spiritual communities aren't built by programs alone. They are formed by meeting people where they are and walking with them into deeper wholeness—building relation*ships.* Spiritual communities grow and thrive when we intentionally intersect with others in relation*ship* and share our common life orbits. Vibrant, growing spiritual communities create and sustain intentional orbits that help people in the church and the community holistically thrive in relation*ship,* disciple*ship,* and leader*ship.*

Thriving disciples form thriving churches. Thriving churches bless and transform broken communities. Thriving churches build thriving communities.

Wrap-Up

The Casting Crowns' song *If We Are the Body* reminds believers that representing Christ means reflecting his compassion, healing, guidance, and outreach in everyday life. The song challenges the church to demonstrate Christ's love in tangible ways and to point others toward him.[54] What might break loose in a church if the leaders actually wrestled with these simple, yet profound questions? Is the life of Jesus and his teachings being lived out in the community in a way that results in transformed people, lives, and communities with Kingdom impact? Is the church a preferred port of call in the community? Why or why not? How is the church disconnected from the *ships* (neighbors) in its harbor (mission field)? What intentional

---

[54] Casting Crowns, "If We Are the Body," on *Casting Crowns,* Beach Street Records, 2003, audio recording.

disciple*ship,* relation*ship,* and leader*ship* orbits does the church invest in for the benefit of all? How is the church dispatching its disciple*ships* to reach, rescue, equip, and love the relation*ships* who are out to sea?

God did not create us simply to survive or to live in isolation—God designed us to thrive in deep connection with God and with one another. From the very beginning, we see this truth in the image of the Triune God: Father, Son, and Holy Spirit living in perfect unity. Made in this divine image, we are inherently relational beings. Yet in our modern world, marked by hyper-individualism, technological dependence, and the erosion of genuine community, many have become disconnected from others and also from purpose, belonging, and spiritual vitality.

The church has a crucial opportunity—and responsibility—to respond. But that response must go beyond Sunday attendance. It must go beyond doing good deeds, and it must include a relational connection. It means fostering holistic human flourishing in line with Christ's example: spiritual vitality, relational health, emotional wholeness, purposeful calling, and physical/material stewardship. It requires a holistic approach to people's well-being and development, including relation*ships,* disciple*ship,* and leader*ship.*

When churches help people reconnect—through meaningful relation*ships*, disciple*ship* including acts of service, and shared life—they become more than struggling or irrelevant religious institutions; they become living expressions of the Kingdom of God. In a fragmented world, the church is called to be a healing presence, forming thriving disciples who bless their communities through love, grace, and truth.

We will explore this in detail in the following chapters.

Key Points

1. We were created for thriving, not just survival. God designed us for deep, fruitful lives in connection with God and one another—modeled after the loving unity of the Trinity (Genesis 1:26, John 17:21).

2. Thriving requires authentic human connection. Isolation, fueled by individualism, technology, and cultural shifts, is eroding our capacity for meaningful relation*ships* and weakening the church's relational fabric.

3. The church must move beyond a Sunday-centric model. Jesus didn't build a weekly event—he built a transformative Kingdom. True disciple*ship* isn't measured by attendance but by daily obedience, spiritual depth, and sacrificial love (Luke 9:23).

4. The hunger for belonging, purpose, and impact is real. People seek community, meaning, and influence, whether through social media, service, or AI companions. The church can either meet these needs or lose its voice, influence, and impact in our disconnected world.

5. False connections through AI or digital life cannot replace real community. AI companions and algorithm-fed relation*ships* may simulate intimacy, but ultimately, they deepen emotional and relational poverty, failing to offer the growth and reciprocity only real human interaction can provide.

6. The church is uniquely positioned to meet people's deepest needs. By fostering a holistic approach that includes belonging (inclusive community), purpose (service and calling), and impact (missional living), churches become agents of healing and renewal in a fragmented society.

7. Jesus modeled and taught holistic thriving. Drawing from his life and teachings, we see five key dimensions of thriving:
   - Spiritual Vitality (relation*ship* with God)
   - Relational Health (loving others well)
   - Emotional Wholeness (internal peace and integration)
   - Purposeful Calling (living with Kingdom mission)
   - Physical/Material Stewardship (embodied faith and care for needs)
8. Thriving disciples build thriving churches. When churches focus on these five dimensions, they cultivate people who don't just attend—they live out their faith in homes, workplaces, and neighborhoods.
9. Spiritual transformation is the true measure of church health. The fruit of healthy discipleship is not buildings, programs, or numbers but transformed lives, resilient relation*ships*, and Christlike character. That's the fruit of healthy disciple*ship*.
10. Churches must meet people where they are to form spiritual communities. Programs can't substitute for presence and relation*ships*. Walking with people through pain, purpose, and daily life is how thriving communities—and movements—are born and grow.

Case Study: The Journey of New Hope Community Church

Background

New Hope Community Church is a mid-sized congregation in a suburban area. For years, their ministry strategy revolved around Sunday services—high-quality worship, engaging sermons, and well-run children's programs. Attendance was steady, but spiritual growth felt stagnant. Leaders noticed that even longtime members were disconnected, and newcomers struggled to integrate beyond the service. After COVID-19, this problem worsened. Many people stopped attending altogether, and those who returned often seemed emotionally distant, spiritually disengaged, and relationally isolated.

The Shift

Prompted by growing concern, the church leader*ship* began to reevaluate what it meant to be a thriving church. They recognized that the "attendance equals health" model no longer worked (if it ever did). Inspired by Christ's holistic vision of human flourishing, they re-centered their ministry around five key dimensions: spiritual vitality, relational health, emotional wholeness, purposeful calling, and physical/material stewardship.

They started small:

- **Spiritual Vitality:** Instead of focusing solely on Sunday messages, they launched midweek "Abide" groups—small gatherings centered on prayer, scripture reflection, and spiritual practices.
- **Relational Health:** They invested in forming diverse, intergenerational small groups and emphasized vulnerability and mutual care rather than just Bible knowledge.
- **Emotional Wholeness:** They offered workshops on mental health, grief, and forgiveness, partnering with local Christian counselors and trauma-informed leaders.
- **Purposeful Calling:** The leader*ship* began asking, "What passions and gifts do our people bring?" They stopped assigning volunteers to predefined roles and

began co-creating ministries with members. One young woman started an art therapy group for trauma survivors; another man launched a weekly handyman ministry for single moms and seniors.

- **Physical/Material Stewardship:** The church began hosting regular food drives, financial literacy classes, and community wellness events. They even added walking groups and fitness classes for holistic care.

The Impact

Within two years, New Hope had not necessarily grown in Sunday attendance, but they had deepened. People who once sat quietly in the back row are now more engaged, leading prayer groups, mentoring teens, and forming unlikely friendships across generations. Isolated retirees found belonging. A young couple recovering from loss found emotional healing. A man on the brink of burnout rediscovered purpose. The church wasn't just "doing church"—they were becoming a family driven by a missional purpose, a Kingdom community marked by love, service, and transformation.

And what began within the walls of the church began to ripple outward. The disciples began serving in city shelters, coaching local teams, and advocating for justice. They brought Christ with them into everyday spaces. People in the community started noticing—not because of a marquee sign, but because of the authenticity and love they encountered in the lives of these disciples.

CHAPTER THREE

The Why and How for Building New Relationships

We are called to offer God's love to everyone,
in order to achieve that unity which does not
cancel out differences, but values
the personal history of each person and
the social and religious culture of every people.[55]

Pope Leo XIV

The Why

Let's first unpack what we mean and don't mean by building "new community." It does not mean the existing church people will be displaced or no longer cared for. It does not necessarily mean launching a new worship experience or a new program. Creating opportunities for new community (relation*ships)* means creating places, spaces, time, energy, focus, and orbits for building new relation*ships* amongst those in your community—your church's mission field or your harbor.

The purpose of building new community is not to increase the Sunday morning attendance, nor is it to gain additional giving units to support the budget. The relation*ship*-building will likely be outside current church programming and outside the facility.

---

[55] Pope Leo XIV, "Let Us Walk Towards God and Love One Another," *Vatican News,* May 2025, https://www.vaticannews.va/en/pope/news/2025-05/pope-leo-xiv-let-us-walk-towards-god-and-love-one-another.html.

The idea of building (new) community is based on a deep, authentic desire to invest in people outside the congregation and beyond individuals' current friend zones. It is an investment and a profound desire to truly grow and know new people. The approach to building new community is bathed in curiosity, listening, vulnerability, and a commitment to being judgment-free, and perhaps even to wandering beyond our current comfort zone (orbits) as a church and as individuals. When this type of community is built, a natural tendency for organic spiritual conversations develop over time.

Neighbor is not a geographic term.
It is a moral concept.[56]

Rabbi Joachim Prinz

This approach to building community is counterintuitive to the methods and practices most church leaders were taught and currently use for church growth. In the mid-twentieth century, the church was central to people, families, and the culture. Church was a common orbit for the vast majority of people. Congregants attended worship every week, were involved in a Sunday school class, served their greater community through the ministries of the church, and their lives intersected with most of their friends, family, coworkers, and neighbors through the life of the church.

In the mid-twentieth century, communities were centered on weekly church attendance and even membership. It was a natural and obvious choice and a part of life for the majority of the population. The church was where people practiced and developed their faith. When other options for community were scarce, the church was also the place where people socialized, learned, networked, served, and were "seen."

[56] Jewish Federation of Greater Hartford, Facebook post, May 31, 2020.

In the late twentieth century, the culture began to shift, starting with the changes in the Blue Laws in the 1960s. Blue laws are state or local laws that restrict or prohibit certain activities, typically on Sundays or other religious holidays. These laws, often with roots in religious observance of the Sabbath, have evolved over time and now primarily regulate alcohol sales and other commercial activities.

Numerous other cultural shifts have affected the church in the past few decades. These shifts have resulted in the church no longer being central in communities or people's lives. People now have countless choices about how to invest their time, dollars, and energy, and where to find community.

Passing judgment on how unchurched or dechurched people "should" spend their time is not helpful and is likely (and oftentimes) damaging. Culture has shifted, and the church has not remained relevant for a growing population. While the church grieves the church-centric culture of the twentieth century, it can no longer create a sense of authentic community and belonging as if the culture has not changed. Opening the doors of the church and "expecting" people to show up (attractional model) like they once did is a nonviable proposition for the postmodern, post-Christian twenty-first century. To become healthy, vital, and missional, churches must move away from the attractional model. Healthy, vital churches root all they do in being relationally and missionally driven—not in the survival of the church.

The practice of building new community is turning the whole idea of church health and vitality inside out. Building new relation*ships*/community is not centered on the church facility or the Sunday morning experience. Because of the general distrust in institutions and perceptions that the church is hypocritical, judgmental, and only interested in people's money, new community will need to be built in new places and new ways. Places outside the church and home (often referred to as "third places") offer neutral spaces that are often more comfortable, relaxed, less guarded, and more open to meaningful conversation and interaction.

Building new community is rooted in relation*ships.* It is about the church and its disciples investing deeply and authentically in the people living in its neighborhoods. Real community begins to build when our hearts begin to break for our neighbors. Think of this new community as a working model of the Kingdom of God. Building new community is an approach to the whole person, a holistic approach. It is deeply caring about and for humankind—the people in the mission field.

Rivers do not drink their own water;
Trees do not eat their own fruit;
The sun does not shine on itself,
And Flowers do not spread their fragrance for themselves.
Living for others is a rule of nature.
We are all born to help each other.
No matter how difficult it is ...
Life is good when you are happy;
But much better when others are happy because of you.[57]

The church finds itself in interesting times. The pandemic required the church to make dramatic, overnight shifts in its ministry. The question of whether to mask or not caused divisions that some churches could not overcome. Differences in polity and theology have created deeper divisions, splits, and declining attendance in many churches. The country is experiencing unprecedented divisiveness and toxicity. There's the right wing and the left wing. There's the so-called "right" and "wrong." Harmony, love, peace, empathy, and tolerance

[57] Anonymous proverb (often misattributed to Pope Francis).

seem to be eluding us. Richard Rohr described our current culture and his thoughts on moving forward:

> *Let's be honest:*
> *Religion has probably never had such a bad name.*
> *Christianity is now seen as "irrelevant" by some,*
> *"toxic" by many, and often as a large part of the problem rather than any kind of solution.*
> *Some of us are almost embarrassed*
> *to say we are Christian because of the*
> *negative images that word conjures in others' minds.*
> *Young people especially are turned off by how*
> *judgmental, exclusionary, impractical,*
> *and ineffective Christian culture seems to be.*
> *We must rediscover what St. Francis of Assisi (1182–1226)*
> *called the "marrow of the Gospel."*
> *It's time to rebuild from the bottom up.*
> *If the foundation is not solid and sure,*
> *everything we try to build on top of it is weak and ineffective.*
> *Perhaps it's a blessing in disguise that*
> *so much is tumbling down around us.*
> *It's time to begin again. In the year 1205,*
> *Jesus spoke to Francis through the San Damiano cross:*
> *"Francis, rebuild my church, for you see it is falling into ruin."*
> *If Jesus himself says the church is falling into ruin,*
> *I guess we can admit it also without*
> *being accused of being negative or unbelieving.*
> *Maybe we have to admit it for anything new and good to happen.*

Richard Rohr[58]

[58] Richard Rohr, "Rebuilding from the Bottom Up," Daily Meditations, Center for Action and Contemplation, May 22, 2022, https://cac.org/daily-meditations/rebuilding-from-the-bottom-up-2022-05-22/.

The Ships' Opportunity

By and large, churches have not kept up or remained relevant with their surrounding culture and therefore find themselves becoming increasingly irrelevant and disconnected from mainstream society. The gap has continued to widen with ...

- Our churchy language versus the secular language.
- The ministries offered versus the ministries the community would likely engage in.
- The age gap between most churched people and the unchurched populations.
- Preference driven by the existing congregation versus the greater community.
- Existing schedules and historical ministries versus flexibility and adaptability to reach new people (relation*ships)* with new methods (orbits).
- The rise in the distrust of church leaders and perceived hypocrisy versus the higher trust levels of yesteryear.

As a result of these gaps and the cultural shifts, the country is swelling with the unchurched, according to a Gallup poll, which reports that only 49 percent of U.S. adults belong to a church, synagogue, or mosque—down a whopping 22 points since 2000. Christians are now a minority population, and we must accept this harsh reality and respond accordingly. The church can no longer continue using ministry practices that were guided by being the Christian majority population when this is no longer a reality.

To regain what Jesus intended for the church to be and do, it must develop a sense of urgency to reach new people for Jesus Christ—even if it means we, the churched people, might become uncomfortable with new approaches or not have our own church and ministry preferences met!

We stand at a defining moment. Changes are coming at us with increasing speed and velocity. Practices of yesteryear and normality are no longer realistic expectations. Both the country and the church find themselves in this liminal space and time. Although we are navigating through an unprecedented era, extraordinary opportunities lie before us.

In the past few years, everyone's world has been turned upside down to various degrees. What most seek is comfort, normalcy, and familiarity. Often, those who are churched seek such refuge in their church and with their church friends. So, to suggest that this is the very moment we need to turn the church inside out sounds ludicrous. However, now is indeed the absolute best time to examine our churches from basement to steeple and turn our churches inside out. The church can choose to embark on a missional journey, guided by the Lighthouse (Jesus), into uncharted waters with a new map. Or the church can choose to hunker down under its revered steeple as the ships pass by on their journey to another harbor with a more preferred port of call.

> *It is good for those who have had the dominant culture position to learn with an attitude of humility and to acknowledge that our dominant posture has often made us arrogant, complacent, entitled, and proud.*
>
> **Jon Tyson and Heather Grizzle**[59]

While the uncertainty and lack of normalcy feel unsettling and uncomfortable, these circumstances offer tremendous opportunities. Methods and expectations of yesterday can

---

[59] Jon Tyson and Heather Grizzle, A Creative Minority: *Influencing Culture Through Redemptive Participation* (Heather Grizzle, November 8, 2016).

be tossed overboard. It is a new day where possibilities and potential are everywhere. We have the opportunity to engage in community, innovation, and care in new, refreshing, and relevant ways. No one is promising the journey will be simple or easy, but we need to embrace new approaches and trust the process of transformation.

> *Leaders should celebrate change and evolution.*
>
> *Yes, change is hard, particularly if you think your organization is managing its current mission and working fairly well.*
>
> *But our world is constantly adapting, as are stakeholders and their needs.*
>
> *We need to constantly adjust and grow to maximize the benefits of our work.*
>
> *Change allows us to innovate and adjust, and no matter how scary it is, it is needed.*
>
> **Patrick Riccards, Driving Force Institute**[60]

We must resist going back to the way we've always done things in the life of the church (which likely wasn't all that effective anyway). Instead, we need to use this time for deep evaluation, soul-searching, and innovation. Perhaps we, too, have been the unperceptive ones in Isaiah's proclamation: "Forget the former things; do not dwell on the past. See, I am doing a new thing! Now it springs up; do you not perceive it? I am making a way in the wilderness and streams in the wasteland" (43:18-19, NIV). Gather some of your church leaders and begin a new conversation using these questions to guide you:

---

[60] Patrick Riccards, "Leaders should celebrate change and evolution," *The Ohio Star*, September 9, 2024, https://www.theohiostar.com/2024/09/09/commentary-riccards-leaders-should-celebrate-change-and-evolution/.

- In what ways is our church effectively forming new community (relation*ships)* and reaching new people?
- What are we in the church hanging onto so tightly that we cannot fully embrace the new thing God is doing in our community (mission field, harbor)?
- What is not working well? What do we need to stop doing so that our resources (time, energy, money, building usage, etc.) can be reallocated for something more missionally effective, such as relation*ships,* disciple*ship,* and leader*ship?*
- In what areas have traditional methods taken precedence over the mission of the church—even the Great Commission?
- Where are our personal preferences and internal relation*ships* driving decisions rather than the mission of making new disciples?
- Is the church more of a museum for the saints, adorned with countless gold plaques, or a hospital for the sick, hungry, isolated, and hurting in your community?
- What is the signature ministry of your church (what is your church known for in the community)?
- If the church were to close tomorrow, would anyone notice? Who? Why? How do you know?
- Is the church focusing first on reaching new people and second on caring for those already gathered? How effective is the approach? How do you define "effective"?
- How does your church regularly deploy itself into the community to serve and build new relation*ships* with the unchurched? How effective is the current approach? What shifts in approach may be needed?
- How many disciple-making disciples are there in the church? How many are being developed each year?

- How is your church developing leader*ship* to serve the church and be deployed into the harbor (mission field)? How is your community being transformed and impacted by your church's deployment of its Christian leader*ship*?

As you begin to process the questions above, you may already feel as though you've been twisted, pulled, tugged, challenged, and even turned inside out! This is indeed difficult, transformational work—yet it is the holy, important work that the church and its disciples are called to do. Below is some wise counsel from a nonprofit center leader:

> *Today's nonprofit needs to look deep within*
> *at current systems and structures that are not working.*
> *In order to be nimble, flexible, and adaptable,*
> *the organization of tomorrow needs to be*
> *thoughtful and self-reflective.*

Robin Cabra, NH Center for Nonprofits [61]

As you continue to process the opportunity before you, let's look at some mentors for inspiration. First, Jesus was an incredible teacher and mentor! He invested deeply in relation*ships* with twelve people. He spent a great deal of time with them, investing in building relation*ships* and trust and equipping them for ministry. He led by example. Did he take them to the temple every Tuesday night for study? No! Instead, they gathered around the table, ate together, and with others. Jesus invested daily in his disciples and taught them through everyday situations, professions, and events such as boating, fishing, weddings, walking/traveling, visiting people in their homes, and at the well in the city center. Were the majority of

---

[61] Nonprofit Fixer, "Nonprofit Leadership and Fundraising Quotes," accessed December 2, 2025, https://www.nonprofitfixer.com/nonprofit-fixer-blog/nonprofit-leadership-and-fundraising-quotes.

people whom Jesus and his disciples spent time with those who gathered regularly at the temple? No! They were tax collectors, thieves, sick, sinners, and social outcasts. Jesus went to them—engaging them in their sacred spaces, homes, events, and times. Jesus intersected with them in their regular, routine orbits of life. Jesus is a great example for a relationally driven model of building a treasured community. How is Jesus' ministry model taught in your church?

Next, let's look at the ministry of the apostle Paul. Paul was the first church planter! It is believed that Paul started fourteen churches (likely more). This does not include the number of additional churches that those fourteen-plus planted churches started. Most of those churches were planted over a ten-year period during which Paul traveled over 10,000 miles (a huge feat given the limited transportation options in those days). During his passage, Paul simultaneously preached and demonstrated how to share faith in the marketplace. He was doing life alongside people who spent the majority of their time (their orbits) in their places of business. The apostle Paul is a superior model of building sustainable, multiplying communities. What does Kingdom multiplication look like in your church?

Now, let's look at the ministry of John Wesley, the founder of Methodism. Wesley did not want disciples to be constrained by buildings. He often preached in the open air because there were no seating limits outside. He preached in public gathering places without pre-published times, often gathering 3,000 or more people. Wesley gave these instructions to Methodists in 1784:

> *Let all our chapels be built plain and decent; but not more expensively than is absolutely avoidable; otherwise the necessity of raising money will make rich men necessary to us. But if so, we must be dependent upon them, yea,*

> *and governed by them. And then farewell to the Methodist discipline, if not Doctrine, too.*[62]

Wesley started a movement primarily led by laity that reached millions, predominantly WITHOUT buildings. What might Wesley have to say today about the building-centric approach to ministry used by most churches?

William Booth was a Methodist lay preacher who founded The Salvation Army and felt called to serve the poor and marginalized in London. Booth spent his early days in ministry as a bi-vocational pawnbroker and preacher. He had a strong drive to be an evangelist. Booth originally launched The Salvation Army in one country, but it had spread to fifty-eight countries by the time he died in 1912. The Salvation Army is currently in 134 countries. Unfortunately, William felt burdened by the denomination's pastorate requirements and limitations, which kept him from his passion for evangelism and led him to leave Methodism and launch The Salvation Army. Booth's leader*ship* is a great example of one's drive and heartbreak for the people in the greater community, as well as the adaptive leader*ship*, grit, and tenacity it took to serve his call and start a whole new movement. How is the culture and deployment of evangelism lived out in your church?

As Jesus, Paul, Wesley, and Booth modeled, the church must reimagine its ineffective approaches in disciple*ship*, leader*ship*, and relation*ships*. The church must shift its approaches to redefine how to "do" church rather than go TO church. Jon Ritner says, "The future requires us to replace our industrial disciple-making approach with one that equips individuals to make disciples outside of our factory's four walls. For that,

---

[62] John Wesley's instructions to Methodists in the U.S. (1784), John James Tigert, *A Constitutional History of American Episcopal Methodism* (Nashville: Publishing House of the Methodist Episcopal Church, South, 1908), 592.

we must restructure our disciple-making pathway by actually reversing its flow."[63]

As you ***sent*** *me into the world,*
so I have ***sent*** *them into the world.*

John 17:18 (CEB)

This John 17:18 verse reminds us that Jesus sent his disciples into the world, not into the temple. It highlights the parallel between Jesus' mission and the mission of his disciples, emphasizing their role as ambassadors of Christ. Likewise, Jesus equipped the disciples, who, in turn, through multiple generations, equipped Jesus' followers to be sent into the world.

When we talk about being **sent,** it helps us understand that we are to cover all corners of the world, not just those that show up at the church's doorstep. We are **sent** online. (Vimeo Livestream indicates that 33 percent of parishioners discovered their church online. Forty-five percent of Americans used an online service in 2021. Of those who watched, 15 percent were not people who normally attended church.)[64] Sent means outside the building. *Sent* means being part of the greater community. *Sent* means doing life in the community with people who are not like us (not Christian, not our age, not our socioeconomic level, not our race, not those who share our interests, etc.) so that we might have a greater understanding of our local culture and context. *Sent* means reallocating our insider asset consumption to a new investment in outside people.

Ships are not designed to sit at the dock in port. Ships are

---

[63] Jon Ritner, *Positively Irritating: Embracing a Post-Christian World to Form a More Faithful & Innovative Church* (100 Movements Publishing, 2020).

[64] Aaron Earls, "Online Services Expanded Reach of Churches During Pandemic." Lifeway Research, October 14, 2021, https://research.lifeway.com/2021/10/14/online-services-expanded-reach-of-churches-during-pandemic/.

built for a purpose and are meant to move. They transport people or resources and are equipped for their intended purpose. As you think about the ships your church has built (relation*ships*, disciple*ships*, and leader*ships),* do they still serve the mission well? Are you missing any ships? Is your church's fleet of ships adequately equipped, appropriately maintained, and supplied with the needed and necessary resources? Are there any outdated manuals or equipment that need updating?

Another opportunity available to churches considering building new community is to rethink "who" is responsible. Pastor-centric churches often expect the pastor to be solely responsible for evangelism, community connections, disciple*ship*, and building new relation*ships* (see Romans 12:1 above). This is not a sustainable model, and it is also not the method Jesus modeled or taught. In addition, note that the rapid growth of early Methodism in the United States was a movement fueled by the laity. One of Wesley's famous quotes says, "Give me one hundred preachers who fear nothing but sin, and desire nothing but God, and I care not a straw whether they be clergy or laymen [women], such alone will shake the gates of hell and set up the kingdom of heaven upon the earth."

According to Roger Finke and Rodney Stark, sociologists and educators, "The dramatic meteoric rise of the Methodists was short-lived. It is important to note that the Methodists began to slump precisely when their amateur clergy were replaced by professionals who claimed episcopal authority over their congregations."[65] Lesslie Newbigin, British theologian, missionary, pastor, and bishop, adds this, "Men are not

---

[65] Rodney Stark and Roger Finke, *The Churching of America, 1776-2005: Winners and Losers in Our Religious Economy* (Rutgers University Press, March 3, 2005).

ordained into the ministerial priesthood in order to remove the priesthood away from the people of God, but to encourage, empower, and equip the priestly people of God for their work in the world." Newbigin adds, "The minister's leader*ship* of the congregation in its mission to the world will be first and foremost in the area of his or her own disciple*ship*, in that life of prayer and daily consecration which remains hidden from the world but which is the place where the essential battles are either won or lost."[66] Clergy-centric churches limit the potential of their ministry and their Kingdom impact when they become primarily dependent on one person.

When we are clergy- and staff-centric, we limit the impact of our laity and the impact our community will receive! Bishop Kennon L. Callahan declares, "The age of the professional pastor is over, and the age of the missional pastor has begun."[67]

Pastors and staff (paid and unpaid ministry leaders) are to identify, recruit, equip, and deploy laity for ministry. "The moment you hand power over to other people, you get an explosion of curiosity, innovation, and effort," says Joshua Cooper Ramo, author, strategist, and American business leader.[68]

Eugene Peterson offers these thoughtful insights: "Within the Christian community, few words are more disabling than 'layperson' and 'laity.'"[69] The words convey the impression—an impression that quickly solidifies into a lie—that there is a two-level hierarchy among the men and women who follow

---

[66] Lesslie Newbigin, *The Gospel in a Pluralist Society* (Grand Rapids, MI: William B. Eerdmans, 1989).

[67] Kennon L. Callahan, *Effective Church Leadership: Building on the Twelve Keys* (San Francisco: Jossey-Bass, 1997).

[68] Joshua Cooper Ramo, *The Age of the Unthinkable: Why the New World Disorder Constantly Surprises Us and What We Can Do About* (Little, Brown and Company, 2009).

[69] Eugene Peterson, *The Jesus Way* (Wm. B. Eerdmans Publishing Co., 2007).

Jesus. Some are trained—sometimes referred to as "the called"—the professionals who are paid to preach, teach, and provide guidance in the Christian way, occupying the upper level. The lower level is made up of everyone else, those whom God assigned jobs as storekeepers, lawyers, journalists, parents, and computer programmers.

> *A future-focused church is one with a clear, commonly understood vision for the future. Accordingly, this also means being a church that believes the next generation is essential to the path forward, helping equip young leaders to one day steward the ministry.*[70]
>
> **Barna, NextGen Simple Mentoring**

Rethinking the "How"

(Excerpt from *Inside Out: Everting Ministry Models for the Postmodern Church)*

Often, churches find themselves in patterns of being unrecognizably stuck. They get stuck in the same ministry and program ruts, in the methods that worked at some point in their history (likely from their heydays), in the same events on the same day every January, and with the same expectations that their neighbors should just show up on Sunday and like what the "church people" like. Many churches are STUCK! Churches need to evert their thinking and their doing. They need to turn themselves inside out.

---

[70] Kay L. Kotan and Michael J. Scott, *Inside Out: Everting Ministry Models for the Postmodern Culture* (Market Square Publishing, 2022).

What does it mean to evert? Evert is defined as to turn outward, to turn inside out, to turn upside down, to reverse, to turn out, to reverse, to rotate, to turn around, to revolve, to move outwards, to move out of the way, or to disrupt. For us, the most accurate meaning for how the church needs to evert is inside out. It is a spot-on descriptor for the church on so many levels.

- The congregation needs to move from inside the church walls to out in the community.
- The relevant activities of the church need to move from inside the facility to out amongst the members of the community.
- The focus and priority of the church needs to move from inside the congregation to out in their mission field.
- The budget of the church needs to be less weighted for the benefit of those on the inside and more on those out in the neighborhood.
- The disciple*ship* of the individual congregants needs to move to more inside transformation that results in transformation out in the community.[71]

The majority of churches must face the reality that, by and large, what they are doing is not working or at least not working well. Church attendance in the United States has been generally decreasing over the past few decades. While some individual congregations have experienced growth, the overall trend shows a decline in both church membership and regular attendance. According to Gallup, only 20 percent of Americans attend church every week, while 57 percent seldom or never attend religious

[71] Kay Kotan and Phil Maynard Scott, *Inside Out.*

services. Pre-pandemic, approximately 3,500 people left the religious congregations every day. That's a rate of 1.2 million walking away from church every year. This does not even address the growing number of generations who have never had a religious affiliation. While each church is unique, leading experts say a church should expect to lose about 10 percent to 15 percent of its members year after year.[72] We won't bore you by dissecting church statistics for days on end; you get the picture. The decline is real. Churches must take notice. Churches must develop a sense of urgency to become more vital, fruitful, and fulfilling of the Great Commission. Churches must be willing to adapt their focus, mindsets, and ministries to reverse the decline.

Rethinking the Financial "How"

With shrinking churches comes shrinking budgets. At the same time, there are different values and priorities when it comes to dollars associated with the different generations. This proves to be true when it comes to church generosity. For example, 72 percent of Boomers give to charity, donating an annual average of $1,212 across 4.5 organizations. On the other hand, 84 percent of Millennials give to charity, donating an average of $481 across 3.3 organizations. Boomers make up nearly 24 percent of the population but account for 43 percent of total U.S. giving. In comparison, Millennials make up approximately 26 percent of the population but account for only 11 percent of giving.[73]

An additional consideration is the changing economics. The

[72] "The State of Church Attendance: Trends and Statistics 2023," ChurchTrac, accessed November 15, 2025, https://www.churchtrac.com/articles/the-state-of-church-attendance-trends-and-statistics-2023.

[73] Heather Mansfield, "6 Generations of Giving: Who Gives the Most and How They Prefer to Give," NPTech for Good, August 4, 2023, https://www.nptechforgood.com/2023/08/04/6-generations-of-giving-who-gives-the-most-and-how-they-prefer-to-give/.

ratio of expenses and income for Millennials versus Boomers is substantial. According to Consumer Affairs, Generation Z has roughly 72 percent less purchasing power than Baby Boomers did in their twenties. Home prices have risen about 1,045 percent since 1973. The cost of public and private school tuition has increased by 177 percent and 158 percent, respectively, since the 1970s. Unlike most other expenses adjusted for inflation, gas prices have actually decreased by 9 percent since 1973.[74]

Tithing patterns have also changed in the past decades. Only 3 to 5 percent of Americans who give to their local church do so through regular tithing. Among families making $75,000+, 1 percent gave at least 10 percent in tithing. The average giving by adults who attend U.S. Protestant churches is about $17 a week. Thirty-seven percent of regular church attendees and evangelicals don't give money to the church.

Yet, interestingly, three out of four people who don't go to church donate to nonprofit organizations. At the same time, there has been a huge spike in nonprofit start-ups. We believe this is due to churches moving away from social entrepreneurship. This shift has led the church to stop reaching the youngest generations, who have a strong desire to make a difference in the world. Therefore, the youngest generations are launching nonprofits to gain the opportunity to make a community impact and to make a difference in the world that was once available to them through their church home.

While most churches are seeing decreases in income and budgets, they are also seeing an increase in expenses. Churches are saddled with older buildings, which increase overhead costs for maintenance and utilities. Often, church facilities fall

---

[74] "Comparing the Costs of Generations," *Consumer Affairs,* accessed November 15, 2025, https://www.consumeraffairs.com/finance/comparing-the-costs-of-generations.html.

into disrepair due to a lack of funding for proper maintenance and preventive measures. The availability of congregants to make the repairs is also shrinking as congregations age. (Pew Research's 2025 Religious Landscape Study indicates that the median congregant's age of mainline Protestants is 59—up from 50 in 2007.[75]) Churches are also struggling with rising staff salaries and increased costs of benefits. These circumstances often lead to minimal (if any) dollars for ministry and, specifically, evangelism. In addition, whereas congregants in the past saw their service as a ministry, many are now expecting remuneration for their efforts.

Because of decreased income and increased expenses, the church must rethink its historical reliance on the offering plate for economic sustainability and its ultimate survival. Many churches have moved to a multi-income stream model for financial viability—no longer relying solely on the offering plate.

Rethinking the "How" via Christian Social Innovation

While some may argue that entrepreneurship is not for churches, entrepreneurship is indeed Wesleyan. Wesley launched a publishing house, orphanages, schools, and hospitals. When there was a community need, the church bridged the gap. In the book John Wesley, Compassionate Entrepreneur: *A Wesleyan View of Business and Entrepreneurship,* the writers describe Wesley's social entrepreneurship as follows:

> *He provided believers with practical guidance and theological foundations for business and entrepreneurship*

---

[75] Pew Research Center, "Age, Race, Education and Other Demographic Traits of U.S. Religious Groups," February 26, 2025, https://www.pewresearch.org/religion/2025/02/26/age-race-education-and-other-demographic-traits-of-us-religious-groups/.

particularly in the context of poverty. We argue that Wesley should be viewed as a compassionate entrepreneur—with the compassion of a liberator and the practice of an entrepreneur, as he encouraged believers to actively participate in economic activities, and recognized entrepreneurship as a sustainable and significant way to empower the poor. Wesley's example challenges the church today as his case study serves as a radical and faithful application of biblical economic teachings on business and entrepreneurship.[76]

Let's review the six indicators of healthy and effective approaches to Christian social innovation (entrepreneurship) from the book *Inside Out:*[77]

1. First and foremost, a congregation must have a big heart for its community. For this to be Christian AND social entrepreneurship, it is not centered around making a profit. Christian social entrepreneurship starts because the church sees that a big part of being the church is bearing the burden for the community, making it a better place to live for the people. It also funds the ministry so that the impact can be compounded.

2. The faith community has made significant progress in shifting from its historical descriptors: a building, Sunday, pastor, and offering-plate-centric. While not all four shifts need to be completed, the congregation as a whole is not stuck in all four traditional models. There is simply not enough energy for leaders to move the congregation out of these deep ruts and live into a brand-new way of being a faith community at the same time.

---

[76] T. J. Moon, Wonsuk Cho, and Jonathan L. Bettis, *John Wesley, Compassionate Entrepreneur: A Wesleyan View of Business and Entrepreneurship* (Franklin, TN: Seedbed, 2018).

[77] Kotan and Scott, *Inside Out.*

3. If the faith community has not yet begun to make any of the shifts to move away from being building-centric, Sunday-centric, pastor-centric, and offering plate-centric, there are enough resources to handle both the traditional desires of the congregation and the innovative ministry to reach new people. This normally means there is a significant number of mature, sold-out disciples with a key staff member or two who will lead the new Christian social entrepreneurship, while the existing traditional "services" provided to the traditional congregation are not disrupted. It can be done, but doing both well is much more difficult to accomplish.

   Unfortunately, churches normally wait until they are desperate before exploring this option. By this time, those mature, sold-out disciples who have the desire and passion to pursue Christian social entrepreneurship (who would have been very helpful in these shifts) have long since left. Remember, the APEs (Apostles, Prophets, Evangelists, Ephesians 4:11-12) are the ones who typically give up trying to live out their ministry within the church and leave. They find they typically have to live out their ministry outside the church.

4. The faith communities that successfully launch Christian social entrepreneurial organizations or initiatives are the ones that are culturally and emotionally competent. They are often diverse spiritual communities that live in the neighborhood. They already do life with the very people they are trying to reach. Therefore, they do not have a large cultural and emotional gap that other congregations with that gap have to first overcome before reaching their neighborhoods. Since the members of the faith community live in the community and are involved in it, they more easily and readily identify the gaps and opportunities in the community where the church can be most helpful and have the greatest impact.

5. Faith communities that become Christian social entrepreneurs have a significant number of humble, mature disciples. These disciples have moved well beyond the church being "what's in it for them" and now understand that instead it is all about "giving away Jesus to others." These disciple-making disciples possess a strong desire to share their faith with others. In addition, they may have an entrepreneurial background or a natural entrepreneurial tendency, and they are likely to have a clergy leader who shares the same passion. In our experience, this often (but not always) means the pastor is either a second-career pastor or not seminary trained.

6. Christian social entrepreneurs are generally more optimistic people. Kenda Creasy Dean offers these insights in her book, *Innovating for Love: Joining God's Expedition Through Christian Social Innovation:*

> *They steward abundance rather than manage scarcity. Innovating for love requires a mindset of abundance and not scarcity. Scarcity tends to dominate modern financial thinking; the shift to an abundance mindset is as much a creative challenge as a financial one. Yet innovating for love requires an economy of abundance. God calls us to steward waterfalls, not ration drinks in a drought.*[78]

Pinching pennies and leading with a scarcity mindset is not only ineffective but also does not put our best foot forward as the church, nor does it represent the abundance of God in our faith. The church does not always represent Jesus well when it is not missionally focused or operates from a place of scarcity. Remember, when a guest interacts with your church, it can affect how a person feels, reacts, and responds to not only your

[78] Dean, *Innovating for Love*, quoted in Kotan and Scott, *Inside Out* (Market Square Publishing), 2022.

church but to churches in general. On The Carey Nieuwhof Leadership Podcast, Dave Ramsey offered this wisdom: "We're not going to walk around telling people we're Christians unless we are the best in the market because we're a bad witness for Jesus when we're substandard."[79]

The church can embrace both ministry and diverse income streams as long as every source of revenue advances the central mission of disciple-making. The church needs to become a vital part of the greater community. When we separate the church from the community, the church becomes insular and loses its relevance and effectiveness in reaching the people in its mission field. A church's commitment to its community is both an investment in the people and for the people because we want to love like Jesus loved.

Any Christian social innovation must be based on a community need, gap, or opportunity that is relationally focused and not purely transactional. Ideally, the chosen social innovation is not already being addressed by another group. Congregational assets are meant to be leveraged to pursue the mission of making new disciples (disciple-making disciples) of Jesus to transform the world—starting with the harbor (the church's mission field). The church's assets are not the congregation's assets but God's assets to be used for God-sized Kingdom impact to reach new people!

Jesus, the Christian social entrepreneur:

When Jesus arrived and saw a large crowd, he had compassion for them and healed those who were sick. That evening his disciples came and said to him, "This is an isolated place and it's getting late.

---

[79] Carey Nieuwhof, "Dave Ramsey on Broke Thinking in the Church, the Ups and Downs of Starting Ramsey in 1992, and How Millionaires Think and Act Differently," The Carey Nieuwhof Leadership Podcast, episode 487, https://careynieuwhof.com/episode487/.

Send the crowds away so they can go into the villages
and buy food for themselves."
But Jesus said to them, "There's no need to send them away.
You give them something to eat."
They replied, "We have nothing here except five loaves
of bread and two fish."
He said, "Bring them here to me."
He ordered the crowds to sit down on the grass.
He took the five loaves of bread and the two fish,
looked up to heaven, blessed them and broke
the loaves apart and gave them to his disciples.
Then the disciples gave them to the crowds.
Everyone ate until they were full,
and they filled twelve baskets with the leftovers.
About five thousand men plus women and children
had eaten.

Matthew 14:14-21 (CEB)

Rethinking the "How" with Emotional and Cultural Competence

To build new community, we must be both emotionally and culturally competent. Otherwise, we may do more damage than good in our attempt to build new relation*ships*. According to dictionary.com, *cultural competence* (CQ) is "the ability to effectively interact with people from cultures different from one's own, especially through knowledge and appreciation of cultural differences. In general, competence means possessing the necessary skill or knowledge to handle a particular situation or task." Cultural competence is the ability to examine various social and cultural identities, understand and appreciate diversity, recognize and respond to cultural demands and opportunities, and build relation*ships* across cultural backgrounds.

Emotional competence (emotional intelligence or EQ), as described by dictionary.com, "refers to an important set of personal and social skills for identifying, interpreting, and constructively responding to emotions in oneself and others." It includes self-awareness, self-management, social awareness, and relation*ship* management. The term implies ease in getting along with others and indicates one's ability to lead and express oneself effectively. Psychologists define *emotional competence* as the ability to monitor one's own and others' feelings and emotions and use this information to guide one's thinking and actions. It is also often referred to as *emotional intelligence.*

The apostle Paul says this about cultural competence:

So here's what I want you to do, God helping you:
Take your everyday, ordinary life—
your sleeping, eating, going-to-work, and walking-around life—and place it before God as an offering.
Embracing what God does for you
is the best thing you can do for him.
Don't become so well-adjusted to your culture
that you fit into it without even thinking.
Instead, fix your attention on God.
You'll be changed from the inside out.
Readily recognize what he wants from you,
and quickly respond to it.
Unlike the culture around you,
always dragging you down to its level of immaturity,
God brings the best out of you,
develops well-formed maturity in you.

Romans 12:1-2 (MSG)

When developing cultural competence, we must be aware of our worldview and develop positive attitudes towards cultural differences. Gaining knowledge of different cultural practices and world views will be essential. Developing skills in communication and cross-cultural interaction will also be critical.

In Romans 15, Paul gives us another lesson in CQ: he explains that he is free to eat, but he is not free to injure another person in what he eats. Personal freedom must always give way to corporate responsibility. To put it another way, the gospel of love demands that we surrender individual liberties for the sake of our brothers and sisters. We see this demonstrated powerfully in the example of Jesus, who gave up his life and freedom for the sake of the world. When we live by this ethic (CQ, EQ, mature disciple*ship*), we create a community marked by warmth and hospitality. But justice, peace, and joy are communal essentials for life in the Kingdom.

Paul Nixon challenges us from his book, *Cultural Competency: Partnering with Your Neighbors in Your Ministry Expedition:*

> *Every church can do work to get more prepared*
> *for the ministry God calls it to!*
> *We sometimes have to learn new languages,*
> *requiring hours of study.*
> *We have to get out into the community,*
> *requiring hours of listening and partnering.*
> *We have to examine our social and racial privilege*
> *in terms of how it blinds us to ourselves and sabotages any*
> *Good News that we seek to advance in the world.*
> *But finally, cultural competency is a Gift of the Spirit.*[80]

---

[80] Paul Nixon, *Cultural Competency: Partnering with Your Neighbors in Your Ministry Expedition* (Market Square Books, February 2021).

Wrap-Up

Building new, relationally driven community starts by building on just one interaction or conversation. It starts with one relation*ship* sharing a common orbit. Repeat. Repeat. Most new relation*ships* in this postmodern, post-Christian world will not start inside the church (the port). The church's ships must be deployed into the seas of life to interact with other ships as they go about their daily activities.

> *The church often makes building new relationships far scarier and complicated than they truly are. Find shared orbits of interest. Be curious. Be open. Be humble. Be vulnerable. Lead with love. Approach each interaction through the lens of God's love and grace.*
>
> *It is clear to me now that God plays no favorites,*
> *that God accepts every person whatever*
> *his or her culture or ethnic background,*
> *that God welcomes all who revere Him and do right.*
>
> **Acts 10:34-35 (VOICE)**

God plays no favorites, so we, as part of the church, can play no favorites to those already gathering in the congregation over our neighbors who do not yet have a relation*ship* with Christ. Remember, the church is no longer the preferred port of call for most ships. The church must become a fleet of ships deployed to pursue the Great Commission, starting with relation*ships*. Disciple*ship* and leader*ship* will come later.

Now that we have explored why a new spiritual community (new relation*ships*) is needed, let's continue our journey of discovery together.

Key Points

1. Creating opportunities for new community is about creating places, spaces, time, energy, and focus for building new relation*ships* within it.

2. The approach to building new community is bathed in curiosity, listening, vulnerability, and a commitment to being judgment-free, and perhaps even to wandering beyond our current comfort zone as a church and as individuals.

3. Creating new spiritual community is both the clergy's and laity's shared responsibility.

4. Multiple shifts in thinking, supporting, and doing will be needed to focus on the urgent need to build a new spiritual community. The "same ol'" approach is not the pathway forward.

5. Building new spiritual community will likely cause discomfort for some of the existing congregation, as it will require a new approach to how leaders invest their time, how church resources are leveraged to increase missional impact, and moving to a deployed movement rather than a comfortable, attractional-focused congregation.

6. Refocusing on the community's passions, needs, opportunities, and gaps will create a better opportunity to build new spiritual community.

7. Building new spiritual community will require those leading to be emotionally and culturally competent to connect with a new demographic that is currently disconnected.

8. Jesus and other Christian leaders modeled the kind of spiritual community people are hungry for today, but it is largely unavailable.

Case Study

In June of 2024, a new church plant began in one of the most dangerous neighborhoods in Kansas City, Missouri. It had no Sunday services, no members, and no programs for traditional outreach. What it did have was a vision: to create a community centered on love, belonging, and hope. Just one year later, in June 2025, 115 people gather weekly at 6:00 p.m. through a canopy emblazoned with the words "Free Prayer" and loud gospel music to find connection in a world that often overlooks them.

The growth of this church is not remarkable for its size or speed, though from zero to 115 is impressive. What makes it truly surprising is who shows up:

- People experiencing homelessness
- Former "church mothers" disillusioned by past spiritual trauma
- Active substance abusers
- Longtime Christians from nearby churches
- Diverse languages, cultures, and generations

This eclectic group comes for the express purpose of finding community. They find acceptance and belonging. They find love and hope. They don't find judgment and expectations to change.

Every Sunday, attendees come seeking more than a service. They come for community—a place where belonging isn't based on belief. Love comes without condition. No one is judged, and no one is pressured to change. Everyone is invited to share, question, and be known.

They sing songs of deliverance and hope, hear a story about Jesus from the Bible, then gather around tables for a shared meal—no barriers between servers and the served. After the meal, the mic is passed freely. Anyone can reflect on the Bible story, and they do—with unfiltered honesty. Theology mixes with testimony: deep reflections on God's love interwoven with confessions of addiction, heartbreak, and resilience. For many, this is the first time in recent memory that they have been heard, understood, and known—a safe space of radical hospitality.

At the heart of it all is a pastor just one year out of seminary—himself in recovery from years of substance abuse. His story gives credibility to those who don't typically trust church leaders. He doesn't preach down to those gathered from a platform. He walks beside the people, listens deeply, and reminds them that grace is real and present.

This is not a church in the traditional Western sense. It's not aiming for perfection, production, or programs. It is a new kind of community (or is it an ancient one?)—one that breaks molds and expectations.

CHAPTER FOUR
New Relation*ship* Orbits

Anyone who meets a testing challenge head-on
and manages to stick it out is mighty fortunate.
For such persons loyally in love with God,
the reward is life and more life.

James 1:12 (MSG)

As we begin to consider new types of spiritual communities, let us be reminded of their description as discussed in Chapter 3. Here's another way to put it:

You're here to be light, bringing out the God-colors in the world.

God is not a secret to be kept.

We're going public with this, as public as a city on a hill.

If I make you light bearers, you don't think I'm going to hide you under a bucket, do you?

I'm putting you on a light stand.

Now that I've put you there on a hilltop, on a light stand—shine!

Keep open house; be generous with your lives.

By opening up to others, you'll prompt people to open up with God,

this generous Father in heaven.

Matthew 5:16 (MSG)

A Need for a Shift in Focus and Priorities

You are likely aware of the statistics that indicate nondenominational churches are growing at a faster rate than denominational churches. For example, the Southern Baptist Convention shrank from 16.2 million members in 2006 to 13.2 million in 2009, and to 3.8 million by 2022.[81] The United Methodist Church had a U.S. membership of over 6.5 million in 1915 when the population was just over 100 million, and has fallen to approximately 3 to 4.5 million (depending on the source) while the U.S. population has blossomed to approximately 350 million.[82] Notice that Methodists made up about 6.5 percent of the population in 1915. However, while the U.S. population has grown three and a half times its size since then, the number of Methodists has declined by nearly half during the same period, representing only about 3 to 4 percent of the population.

It is important for us to understand why the number of mainline Protestants is declining and nondenominational churches are growing. What could we learn from comparing the approaches of yesteryear to a refreshing relation*ship*-based approach to build new spiritual communities? What insights might we gain from understanding why mainline churches are declining while more nondenominational churches are growing?

Thom Rainer identified five reasons why he believes nondenominational churches are growing in his blog post on *Church Answers*.[83] In summary, those five reasons are as follows:

---

81 Rainer, "Five Reasons Why Nondenominational Churches Are Growing."

82 Walter Fenton, *"The Future of the United Methodist Church, Part III,"* Juicy Ecumenism, March 25, 2025, https://juicyecumenism.com/2025/03/25/future-united-methodist-church-part-iii/; UMData (General Council on Finance and Administration of The United Methodist Church), UMData, https://www.umdata.org/.

83 Rainer, "Five Reasons Why Nondenominational Churches Are Growing."

1. Nondenominational churches tend to be more evangelistic.
2. Nondenominational churches typically invest more financially in reaching their communities.
3. Compared to denominational churches, nondenominational churches are usually less entangled in conflict.
4. Nondenominational churches do not carry the "name" baggage that a denominational church might carry.
5. Nondenominational churches tend to be newer churches that grow faster than older denominational churches.

In reviewing the list above, which stated reasons resonate with you as a church leader? Which ones might ring true for your denominational congregation? What insights have you gained that might be helpful as you consider what shifts would need to occur for your church to focus on investing in new relation*ships* with people in your mission field? To build new spiritual community?

One helpful shift in focus is moving from a scarcity mindset to an abundance mindset. Too often, we allow the natural tendency to concentrate on what we don't have rather than what we do have. The shift needed is to focus on what is possible rather than seeing only obstacles. This approach is not simply wearing rose-colored glasses—indeed, not! Rather, it is digging deeper, looking further, observing where God is already at work, and coming alongside to live into God's preferred future.

Sometimes, we must first simply get out of our own way, such as:

- Escape the deep ruts of doing things simply because we've always done them that way.

- Stop repeating the same ineffective decisions while also expecting a different outcome.
- Halt the drift of the congregation's relevance from its community's context.
- Discontinue the deeper concern for keeping the already-gathered people comfortable at the expense of the mission field.
- Resist the temptation to avoid conflict.
- Cease the reluctance to engage in accountability and ministry assessments.

Another detrimental aspect of a scarcity mindset has emerged with the financial challenges affecting many churches: "We can't do that because we don't have the money," "because we don't have the staff," "because our facility is inadequate." This "why we can't" mindset, rather than a healthier "Why not?!" mindset, immobilizes a church.

Capturing the Spirit of Innovation

Typically, new, innovative ideas or concepts emerge on the fringes of culture and society. New movements start on the fringes with a few passionate leaders and small groups. Rarely is a new movement birthed in the mainstream. There is a natural tendency for existing groups, institutions, and mainstream norms to resist something new that goes against the grain. Innovations challenge the current comforts and traditions, and the mere survival of the organization or institution. For these reasons alone, it is much more likely and possible for something brand new to happen outside the cultural norms and traditions as well as within institutions. Conversely, the resistance is low or even nonexistent on the fringes.

When launching something new, it is also important to understand the difference between adaptation and innovation.

"One of the key differences between innovation and adaptation is that innovation is voluntary. Adaptation is not."[84] Renowned economist, Theodore Levitt, stated it this way, "Creativity is thinking up new things. Innovation is doing new things." Our culture is starving for innovative approaches to spiritual communities.

To launch a new kind of spiritual community, the church will have to be innovative, not adaptive. Innovation calls out into the wild frontier or the depths of the remote seas. Think of it as having the same kind of spirit as astronauts, Lewis and Clark, the first American settlers, the Gold Rushers, those who plunge into the depths of the sea to explore new life, and those who climb Mount Everest. Innovators seek transformation long before it becomes a necessity. Innovators are dreamers, not just for the sake of dreaming but because they believe there is always something more we are called to do and to become. Innovation is born from a driving passion and commitment. It's something innovators absolutely must do! Innovators are not satisfied with the status quo. They have a deep-seated drive and wiring to constantly create, invent, revolutionize, and chart new paths for a better tomorrow for their fellow humans. Adapting gets us through today. Innovation brings us better tomorrows.

Innovative spiritual communities do not emerge from a programmatic approach, nor do they come from a required task or responsibility. Innovative spiritual communities are deeply invested in knowing and loving the people in their community. It is often tied to a need, desire, gap, or opportunity of the people you're currently building (or hoping to build) new relation*ships* with. In other words, an authentic

---

[84] Carey Nieuwhof, "The 5 Kinds of Church Leaders We're Seeing Right Now (and their Future Prospects), Carey Nieuwhof, https://careynieuwhof.com/the-5-kinds-of-church-leaders-were-seeing-right-now-and-their-future-prospects/.

spiritual community is a movement guided by one's heart, not a movement guided by only one's mind or the church calendar.

Entrepreneurs used to make up a larger percentage of mainline churches' congregations. By and large, people with an entrepreneurial spirit are either not attracted to or do not stay with organizations that are unimaginative. Consequently, the number of people remaining in most churches who have the natural capacity to think creatively, take risks, and launch new ventures is growing increasingly sparse. Yet, Pastors & Entrepreneurs partnered with Barna and found that small business owners are trusted twice as much as churches.[85] Church leaders, an abundance attitude will lead you to recognize the opportunities this study reveals. On the other hand, steer clear of a scarcity mindset that might lead you to believe there is no point in launching any innovation because of a lack of trust in the church.

And here is some great news: seven out of ten Americans believe partner*ships* between pastors and entrepreneurs can solve the world's greatest problems! The vast majority of entrepreneurs want to use their talents to serve God, but 62 percent lack the understanding of how to do so.[86] Hear this awesome news again, church leaders. Seventy percent of Americans believe that if church leaders and entrepreneurs joined forces, they could solve the world's greatest problems. Not just any problem, but the GREATEST issues plaguing the world. And, if a high percentage of people believe it is possible, imagine the type of support and resources they would offer if such an innovative vision were cast with a solution for one of the world's greatest problems!

---

[85] Pastors & Entrepreneurs, "Research," Pastors & Entrepreneurs, accessed November 18, 2025, https://pastorsandentrepreneurs.org/research/.

[86] Pastors & Entrepreneurs, "Research."

For the most part, entrepreneurs in your community remain untapped. Building relation*ships*, forming partnerships, and dreaming together for greater Kingdom impact must become a more common approach for church leaders. Church leaders will likely need some training or mentoring to travel this pathway, but those resources are available. The real first step, although the most difficult, is to step out of our churchy comfort zones and lock arms boldly and courageously with entrepreneurs. Then, together, explore innovative and different ways to build new relation*ships* and have a greater missional impact.

The Needed Spiritual Communities and Models

In Chapter 1, we explored the culture, context, and statistics for why new spiritual communities are needed. In addition, we identified specific groups with deep and wide needs and desires for spiritual community. As you begin to discern what type of new relation*ships* you, your church leaders, and individual congregants have the capacity, gifts, and desire to reach, you will begin the journey of determining the best way to build those new relation*ships*.

To build new spiritual community, many may need to first make a mental shift. Too often, we believe that meeting another's needs is the endgame (e.g., providing food or clothing) rather than just the start. As a rule, the common approach has been transactional. Because of this common practice, the vast majority of churches have not invested relationally in their community. Yes, we are absolutely called to feed the poor, clothe the naked, care for the sick, and so on. Yet this is just the beginning—not the endgame. It is through meaningful interaction with people who meet those needs that holistic ministry occurs.

Ministry is a contact sport—relational contact.

Transactional ministry makes us feel good, but it negates the much-needed human and spiritual components. The receiver does not have the opportunity to experience the spiritual and human aspects of the gesture. The "giver" misses the opportunity to serve, develop relation*ships,* love as God loves us, and mature in their own disciple*ship* journey. Providing goods and services (e.g., clothing, food, and building houses) offers a pathway to connect with people and build relation*ships.* Connecting with those you are in ministry with is where relation*ships,* friend*ships,* and spiritual community are born—and a place where a disciple*ship* journey may begin.

Authentic spiritual community emerges when the gifts, resources, experiences, passions, and wisdom of disciples—both clergy and laity—intersect with the needs, gaps, and opportunities within the broader community. Such spiritual communities are formed as disciples actively engage their God-given spiritual gifts and life experiences, viewing others with the eyes of a disciple and a heart full of love. In doing so, they build new relation*ships* and respond meaningfully where needs are unmet and opportunities arise.

There are thousands of ways to build new spiritual community. As a church or an individual disciple, choose one specific area to start. Believe it or not, having one key area of focus will bring about more Kingdom impact and transformation than multiple areas of focus. One key focus area (e.g., demographic, cause, issue, gap, problem, opportunity) provides clearer messaging, resource alignment, and the best leverage opportunities. The same is true for individuals. However, think about the potential community impact a deployment of several disciples from your church could have. Each disciple could be creating a new spiritual community in their giftedness sweet spot, resulting in multiple new spiritual communities. Check out Kotan's book in *The Greatest Expedition* series titled *Expanding the Reach Through Marketplace Multipliers*[87] to explore how to deploy disciples into the community for ministry.

Let's take a deeper look at how new spiritual community with the demographics identified in Chapter 1 can be built to first meet the immediate needs (and eventually much more). You will also find various models that new spiritual communities and social/spiritual entrepreneurs are building to bridge community gaps, needs, desires, or opportunities.

Community with Mothers

In Chapter 1, statistics and studies were cited regarding the unmet needs and desires of mothers. As you remember, mothers reported a lack of parenting support, did not feel valued by the church, were not being invited to the table for decisions related to parenting and family, felt anxious and exhausted, and more. Nearly 80 percent of mothers reported that they would value a way to connect with other mothers outside of work and home. And remember, mothers typically have the greatest influence on their children's spiritual lives.

How is your church supporting and equipping mothers in your community? What percentage of your mission field consists of mothers who are currently raising children? What are the specific needs and desires of the mothers in your context? You will likely need to engage in conversations with mothers to be deeply responsive to their specific needs, gaps, and desires in your context. Make no assumptions. Gather the facts. Be curious. Listen—before any plans are made.

---

[87] Kay Kotan, Wayne Schmidt, and Carrie Whitcher, *Expanding the Reach Through Marketplace Multipliers*, vol. 14 in *The Greatest Expedition* series (Market Square Books, 2021).

Who in your congregation has a passion for supporting mothers and has the giftedness to connect with them? How can the church support, encourage, and deploy your congregant(s) to build new spiritual community with mothers? Remember, stay away from a program approach. This is the church's default mode. Instead, think relation*ships*—building new relation*ships*. Through relation*ship*-building, you will gain trust and a deeper understanding of how best to journey alongside mothers in your community.

Here are some ideas to help spark your imagination to begin building relation*ships* with mothers:

- Rather than simply providing a diaper pantry for young mothers, provide an opportunity for those mothers receiving the diapers to connect. Invite community partners to offer workshops or presentations (e.g., budgeting, cooking, parenting, organizing) to benefit mothers based on the needs, gaps, issues, and opportunities identified in your earlier conversations.
- Offer one-on-one mentoring to young mothers who may not have family around for support and assistance.
- Offer gatherings where empty-nest mothers and grandmothers can pour into young mothers by offering support, a listening ear, and sharing tips, experiences, and strategies.
- Provide a mother's night out to give mothers a much-needed break.
- Provide a mother's retreat experience, pampering mothers with massages, yoga, pedicures, styling tips, prayer, and more. Often, community business partners will offer their services (complimentary or reduced fees) to promote their businesses or give back to their community.
- Offer complimentary childcare during these gatherings if needed/desired by the mothers.

- Ensure mothers are present, have a voice, and are heard at your church's decision-making table. This will require an understanding of their timetable and family rhythms, and the ability to accommodate those schedules.
- Refocus the existing children's ministry to a holistic family approach rather than a segregated community. Provide modern, relevant, and accessible resources to equip mothers as spiritual leaders in their homes.

Community With Young Adults

Many of those in the younger generations experienced the COVID-19 pandemic during some of their most formative years. For example, when the developmental need and desire for social connection with peers were at their peak, teenagers found themselves isolated from their friends. Young adults experienced the cancellation of monumental life events such as graduations, weddings, and baby showers. Activities and hobbies had to be abandoned or greatly modified. To complicate matters, these youth and young adults often lacked the guidance and support from parents who were also trying to navigate this unprecedented time.

Younger generations highly value safety, authenticity, and transparency. They are hungry for community and are seeking purpose and meaning in their lives. They have little to no trust in institutions. Remember, Springtide reports that young people from ages thirteen through twenty-five are three times more likely to have been hurt by organized religion than to trust it. Therefore, the approach to youth and young adults is not finding the right (magic) program to launch. Planning ministry and expecting young people to show up is not the way forward in this post-pandemic, postmodern world.

Connecting with younger generations is about showing up, being vulnerable, listening well, and refraining from judgment.

Again, the approach needs to be highly relational and authentic. But it will take time to build spiritual relation*ships* because trust must be won first. Unfortunately, the mistrust from these young people has been frequently justified in the institutional church, church leaders, and people who call themselves Christians. To build a spiritual community with younger generations, we will have to go to their spaces of comfort. We can't expect them to come to ours.

Here are a few sparks of inspiration to help you begin building relation*ships* with youth and young adults:

- Attend and support sporting and extracurricular events at your local high school. Over time, build relation*ships* with the students, coaches, sponsors, and teachers. Discover meaningful ways in which you can support and encourage students.
- Volunteer your time and talents to an organization or school in your area that serves the youth. By sharing your time and talents, the youth will be more open to you and to opportunities to build trusting relation*ships*.
- Connect with your local high school or college entrepreneur tracks or your community's business incubation center. Teachers are often looking for case studies, entrepreneurs, and business leaders who will invest time and wisdom with their students. You will often find a social thread within many entrepreneurial dreams and endeavors that might ignite a future partnership.
- Offer to be a mentor (or just hang out with) a young adult who is on a similar path as yours. This could be at your workplace, in the greater community, during a shared activity, or through a community organization. Find commonalities to build relational bridges.
- Because younger generations are still finding their footing in life, connect with them by providing

tools to help them in the places, experiences, and understandings they are seeking (not our agenda but theirs). They appreciate resources that help them better understand themselves and gain insights into their life's purpose and meaning.

- Join them (or create) a digital gaming room. Participate in the activities they love and create opportunities for conversation and connection.
- In Kay's work with Kenda Creasy Dean, a collection of stories from social entrepreneurs was compiled. Dean wrote one of the books in Kotan's curated *The Greatest Expedition* series titled *Innovating for Love.*[88] One of the video stories features a completely fresh approach to youth ministry. Check out the short interview in our Resource Hub with Matt Overton from The Forge.[89]

Community Connected with Mental Health

There are a couple of approaches to consider if you feel called to build a new spiritual community connected to the mental health crisis. One approach is to build overall awareness and offer support and resources to promote mental health in your community. Another approach is to concentrate on the mental health struggles of one demographic (e.g., teenagers) or a particular type of mental health struggle (e.g., those suffering from feelings of anxiety or isolation). Remember, neither of these approaches is meant to be a substitute for services provided by mental health professionals. Instead, these approaches are relation*ship*-based to support the intention of having a positive impact on mental health in your community. And, once again, there is a tremendous opportunity for collaborative partnerships

88 Dean, *Innovating for Love.*

89 Interview may be accessed at www.kaykotan.com under "Resources" and then selecting the "Resource Hub."

with the mental health professional community.

As we lean into the research covered in Chapter 1, we must remember the intriguing statement from former Surgeon General Dr. Jerome Adams, in which he argued that the country can't completely treat its way out of the mental health crisis "since only 20% of health is actually addressed in a doctor's office. The rest of what impacts human health, including mental health, is what happens in communities. The other 80% happens in communities that are connected, that are supportive of women and minorities, that have childcare, that have good educational opportunities, that have a good-paying job, or both. And I think we need to really focus on building those stronger communities."[90]

Yes, the church can focus on building stronger communities—new spiritual communities. If your church and/or a few leaders feel called to be involved in mental health ministry, begin by identifying a niche demographic or a specific segment of the mental health crisis in your community. As agents of social holiness, we, as the church and as disciples of Jesus, must help find (and advocate for) solutions and offer hope and love to our neighbors suffering from mental illness. The church needs to be a part of helping communities build awareness (even within the church), offer support, and find pathways to improved mental health.

Here are some thought-starters to fuel your thinking and help you begin building relation*ships* within the mental health community:

- If there is a need in your community, launch a grief support group. There are many resources available to help you get started.

---

[90] Christensen, "Mental Health Crisis Could Undermine Our Democracy."

- Sponsor workshops or speakers to address a key area of mental health concerns in your community. Design next steps of support and community in coordination with the facilitator or speaker. Invest relationally with the workshop or speaker-event attendees.
- Meet with your local mental health providers. Ask them how the church can assist and provide a positive impact on mental health in the area. Co-create next steps and a relational follow-up approach.

Consider modifying these two successful approaches for your context, or perhaps it sparks your imagination for another approach:

- Identifying the need for improved mental health of college students, a new relational ministry was born. Starting with a used bus, those involved in the Struggle Bus ministry parked at a local college and offered support, resources, and a space to decompress on the Struggle Bus. Check out the video interview with its founder in our Resource Hub.[91]
- Due to a significant need in their community, Cornerstone Church in Michigan launched a support center that includes support groups, professional counseling, financial coaching, and Stephen Ministry. Partnering with licensed professionals and equipped laypeople, the church is committed to helping people navigate their search and ensuring finances are never prohibitive in their search for healing.

Community With the Nones

With the vast majority of Americans reporting that they are spiritually open, there is a great opportunity to build new

---

[91] www.kaykotan.com.

spiritual community. However, we must rethink our approach and expectations of former times. We must again go to this community rather than expecting it to show up at the church or to have any interest in our current ministries. If this were going to happen, it would have likely already happened. We must be a deployed people whose hearts break for those who do not yet have a relation*ship* with Christ or a spiritual community to connect with, share with, and grow with. Again, we must forgo any expectations of building a new spiritual community as the solution to saving or growing the church. Instead, this must be a Kingdom-focused, heart-driven, relational approach.

In Chapter 1, we learned that the Nones desire warm, friendly encounters and involvement in social causes. But even these top desires of the Nones have a much lower score compared to those who are practicing Christians. To connect with the Nones, we must recognize that many of them distrust organized religion and its leaders, see the church as irrelevant to their daily lives, and perceive it as overly judgmental and preoccupied with money. There is much to overcome, so a different approach is required.

Here are ideas that we hope will ignite creativity to begin building relation*ships* with the Nones:

- Start with your neighbors. Invite neighbors to your home for a game night. Host a barbecue potluck in your driveway. Launch neighborhood tailgating parties at the local high school or college football games. Host a neighborhood corn hole, lawn darts, or croquet tournament in your neighborhood cul-de-sac or local park.

- Find places to connect repeatedly in your community where unchurched people hang out and do what you also like to do. These activities might be golfing or pickleball, playing cards, or volunteering at the school or community organization. Over time, build relation*ships,* earn trust, and have the opportunity to have spiritual but not religious conversations. "Always be prepared to give an answer to everyone who asks you to give the reason for the hope that you have" (1 Peter 3:15, NIV).

- Become gracefully curious. Demonstrate sincere interest in people. Notice something about them that you can compliment them on or connect with them through (e.g., a person is wearing clothing that highlights a particular team or destination you also support or like). Ask more questions and listen more than you talk. Remember, this is an investment in connecting within God's Kingdom, not working towards a church invitation (or even an expectation). It is an authentic, heart-driven investment in knowing and loving God's people.

Consider modifying this successful approach for your context, or perhaps it sparks your imagination for another approach:

- One Christian social entrepreneur established new spiritual community connections through The Kitchen Collective. This innovation connects the Nones in the community and offers a whole new level of community entrepreneurism through a modern, shared commercial kitchen, retail, and event space.

Resources for Church and Organizational Leaders

If you find yourself stuck or just need some assistance, the following resources and organizations are helping leaders build new relation*ships* and boldly launch new spiritual communities.

Hopeful Neighborhood Project

Reverend Doctor Tony Cook launched the Hopeful Neighborhood Project. The Hopeful Neighborhood Project "exists to help you break through that awkwardness, so you can create the type of neighborhood where everyone knows each other and works together to actively pursue the common good."[92] They focus on the neighborhoods' strengths (not what's wrong) and work with neighbors using their gifts and uniqueness. The Hopeful Neighborhood Project helps churches imagine new possibilities and create a "Neighborhood Action Plan." Rev. Cook states, "The Message of truly knowing and loving one's community isn't just attractive; it calls us back to one of the strongest commands of Christ."

The Wellbeing Project

Launched in 2014, the Wellbeing Project[93] was a co-creation of nonprofits, intermediaries, foundations, universities, media groups, venture capital firms, museums, art institutions, and more. Their purpose is to create cultural and systemic change to address dysfunction and high burnout rates across the social change sector. Institutional dysfunction, absence of inner well-being, toxic work environments, lack of trust, bullying, discrimination, and dysfunctional power dynamics were all cited as issues contributing to the dysfunction and burnout.

The Wellbeing Project supports social entrepreneurs and nonprofit leaders who are struggling with their health and relation*ships*. Among other things, their program helps leaders gain a new understanding of well-being and assists them with healthier work and life patterns.[94] The theme of their

---

92 The Hopeful Neighborhood Project, https://www.hopefulneighborhood.org/.

93 The Wellbeing Project, https://wellbeing-project.org/.

94 *Stanford Social Innovation Review*, "Integrating Individual and Organizational Well-Being," accessed November 15, 2025, https://ssir.org/articles/entry/integrating_individual_and_organizational_well_being.

2024 Annual Report, "Locally Rooted, Universally Human," showcases the transformative power of local well-being approaches. They describe their mission this way: "Being part of a movement is personal, aspirational, and rooted in hope. At its heart, the wellbeing movement for social change reflects optimism—an unyielding belief that change is possible."[95]

The Good Neighbor Experiment

Launched in Wichita, Kansas, in 2015, the nineteen-week, hands-on cohort, the Good Neighbor Experiment, was created by the nonprofit The Neighboring Movement out of a desire to live out their faith within the context of a neighborhood. After years of researching and experimenting, they now assist churches in fostering long-term relation*ships*, focusing on the gifts of neighbors, and following joy toward authenticity. In short, the "Key Ingredients of Neighboring (KIN) are joy, relation*ship*, and abundance."

The Neighboring Movement shares its purpose:

> *We believe that an asset-based approach to neighboring can create lasting change in the world, reduce a host of social issues, and increase the quality of life for individuals, communities, and beyond.*
>
> *We achieve our "Big Idea" by living out relation**ship**, abundance, and joy in our founding neighborhood and sharing what we've learned in simple, doable, and universal ways with individuals, churches, and civic organizations.*[96]

---

[95] The Wellbeing Project, "Locally Rooted, Universally Human: 2024 Annual Report," The Wellbeing Project, accessed November 16, 2025, https://wellbeing-project.org/2024-annual-report/.

[96] The Neighboring Movement, accessed November 18, 2025, https://neighboringmovement.org/.

The Other Significant Others

The book The Other Significant Others by Rhaina Cohen[97] came from her concerns around a 2021 study, "The State of American Friendship: Change, Challenges, and Loss."[98] The study revealed alarming statistics about the decline of Americans' friendship circles. In her 2024 interview about her book, Cohen shares, "This friendship recession is particularly bad for men. The percentage of men with at least six close friends has fallen by half since 1990, from 55 percent to 27 percent. The study also found the percentage of men without any close friends jumped from 3 percent to 15 percent, a fivefold increase."[99] As a further friendship concern, Cohen referenced the U.S. Surgeon General's loneliness study, in which Dr. Vivek H. Murthy claimed the country is experiencing an "epidemic of loneliness."[100]

In her book, Cohen explores the question (originally the topic of an article), "What if friendship, not marriage, were at the center of American Life?" She builds on the subject in her book by reimagining life with friendship at the center. This is a great resource when leaders are shifting their thoughts, ideas, and beliefs about relation*ships* and friendships. If friendship, in addition to marriage, were at the center of your church's life, what would change about the way you build community? How

---

97 Rhaina Cohen, *The Other Significant Others: Reimagining Life with Friendship at the Center* (New York: Random House, 2024).

98 American Survey Center, "The State of American Friendship: Change, Challenges, and Loss," accessed November 18, 2025, https://www.americansurveycenter.org/research/the-state-of-american-friendship-change-challenges-and-loss/.

99 American Survey Center, "Reimagining Friendships in Everyday Life," accessed November 18, 2025, https://www.americansurveycenter.org/newsletter/reimagining-friendships-in-everyday-life/.

100 Office of the U.S. Surgeon General, *Our Epidemic of Loneliness and Isolation: The U.S. Surgeon General's Advisory on the Healing Effects of Social Connection and Community* (Washington, DC: U.S. Department of Health and Human Services, 2023).

might your ministries, small groups, and outreach reflect the value of deep, covenant-like friend*ships* as vital expressions of disciple*ship?*

A Crisis of Disciple*ship*

Pastor John Mark Comer is convinced that America is experiencing a crisis of disciple*ship*. And we agree wholeheartedly! His wisdom and insights in his podcast with Carey Nieuwhof speak to how the church is missing the mark in connecting with people and helping them grow in their disciple*ship*. In the podcast, Comer shared, "I am more and more convinced that the future of the church is smaller. It's around tables, not stages. It's relational. It's formational. It's prayer-based."[101] Comer's podcast is a great starting point in helping church leaders begin to peel back and reveal the relation*ship* and disciple*ship* gaps between the church and its community.

Wrap-Up

For most churches and Christians, the hardest part of building new spiritual community is letting go. Letting go of past methods that are no longer relevant or effective. Letting go of our preconceived notions about what nonreligious people think, feel, or need. Letting go of our own comfort. Letting go of the idea that we just need to find that next new program and the church will return to its former heyday. Letting go of the presumption that the primary means of church growth is by people showing up on Sunday. Letting go of the notion that church vitality is measured by the number of butts in the pews and the bucks in the offering plate. Letting go of the erroneous

---

[101] Carey Nieuwhof, "John Mark Comer on the Crisis in Discipleship, Why Weekend Sermons and Services Aren't Resonating, Determining Your Real Motives, and Why He's No Longer Traveling and Speaking," The Carey Nieuwhof Leadership Podcast, episode 626, accessed November 18, 2025, https://careynieuwhof.com/episode626/.

belief that people will come to us rather than understanding that we must once again become a deployed movement. Let go so that God can do a new thing with and through you!

> *Forget about what's happened;*
> *don't keep going over old history.*
> *Be alert, be present.*
> *I'm about to do something brand-new.*
> *It's bursting out! Don't you see it?*
> *There it is!*
>
> **Isaiah 43:18-19 (MSG)**

Just like other relation*ships* (e.g., friends, life partners), building new spiritual community takes time, intentionality, and investment for it to build and grow. Your first attempt may not prove to be fruitful; that is perfectly fine. Evaluate what worked, what didn't, and what you learned from it. Apply your new insights and try again. Fail forward. Don't give up. This is holy work! Building an authentic community is a part of a disciple's focus, call, formation, and work. Our culture is spiritually hungry. As disciples, we must invest with a sense of urgency in answering this desperate call.

Key Points

1. Building new spiritual community takes innovation, not adaptations or tweaks to existing methods or ministries.
2. Building new spiritual community is both a clergy and laity endeavor. It is a collaborative approach.
3. Building new spiritual community will likely be uncomfortable.
4. Building new spiritual community happens on the fringes, not at the core of the institutional church.

5. Building new spiritual community starts with vulnerability, humility, curiosity, and a genuine desire for people to have a relation*ship* with Christ.

6. Building new spiritual community can take numerous forms, but it must be grounded in relation*ships* and based on community needs, desires, gaps, or opportunities.

7. Building new spiritual community is often created by deployed disciples rather than a program or congregation.

8. Building new spiritual community is a process of experimentation, learning, refining, and persistence.

Case Study

The Table and Children's Table[102] is a holistic ministry approach to childcare. The Table is a unique postmodern movement of faith communities desiring to reach younger generations through integrated micro-communities. Planters can use The Table approach to launch a whole new spiritual community, and existing churches can use it to plant a new spiritual community within the existing church (a "both/and" approach). This creates the focus, intentionality, and space for something new to be born without disrupting the current traditions and preferences of the existing congregation.

The Table model involves some significant shifts from traditional models. The Table model shifts disciple*ship* back to the family. The model significantly reduces the traditional cost of paid church staff for a worshiping community and shifts

---

[102] The Creation Incubator, The Table, accessed November 19, 2025, https://creationincubator.org/thetable.

the activity and expectation away from "receiving on Sunday" toward a community of discipling throughout the week. The Table model shifts worship to be much more experiential, relational, non-location-specific, and non-day-specific, with participants literally gathered at "The Table." It moves the faith community towards greater community orientation, relational focus, and laity-driven and laity-led leader*ship.* The model mobilizes the church in its thinking and doing and prioritizes disciple-making. The Table moves the church away from being Sunday-centric, building-centric, and pastor-centric and shifts it away from preference-driven to missionally driven. Finally, The Table model significantly shifts the hours congregants are invested in serving on Sunday to serving in a wider variety of ways that more effectively serve a greater number of people and the mission.

Wrapped inside The Table model is the potential for a full-time children's learning center, The Children's Table, which includes an intentional integration model to reach younger families. This model closes the gap in the church's ability to reach this demographic by providing a service families desperately need—especially given the current child-care crisis[103] (high costs, staffing shortages, limited availability, and the financial impact on the workforce estimated at over $122 billion annually in lost earnings, reduced productivity, and decreased tax revenue).[104]

The Children's Table is built on a five-pillar holistic

[103] First Five Years Fund, "How a Lack of Affordable Child Care Impacts the Economy," March 2025, accessed November 19, 2025, https://www.ffyf.org/resources/2025/03/how-a-lack-of-affordable-child-care-impacts-the-economy/.

[104] Strong Nation, "$122 Billion: The Growing Annual Cost of the Infant-Toddler Child Care Crisis," February 2, 2023, https://www.strongnation.org/articles/2038-122-billion-the-growing-annual-cost-of-the-infant-toddler-child-care-crisis.

approach, which includes experiential learning development, social-emotional development, leader*ship* development, familial spiritual development, and administration and business development. This holistic approach is centered on students and the entire family. When a child enrolls in the Children's Table learning center, the whole family is "enrolled" by being embraced in care, support, and spiritual development.

Some of the keys in this model are as follows:

- Understanding the business model of a childcare center and how it impacts the church and the greater community
- How the practice of undercutting the childcare market has contributed to the childcare crisis
- Understanding how to intentionally integrate the families of the childcare centers and preschools into the spiritual community
- How to provide the resources and tools parents and caregivers desire to become faith leaders in their homes
- Understanding the demographics of the preschool and childcare center workforce and the importance of offering spiritual community for this often spiritually disconnected demographic

The Table and Children's Table ministry model eliminates many of the barriers churches and young families face. Through its five-fold approach, holistic design, intentional integration, comprehensive ready-to-launch blueprint, abundant resources, the additional income stream, coaching, and support, The Table and Children's Table model addresses the common obstacles most churches face when it comes to connecting with younger families: providing safe childcare, providing preschool education, engaging in sound business practices, producing an additional revenue stream, addressing the childcare crisis, and offering relevant spiritual pathways for families in the community.

The book *Inside Out: Everting Ministry Models for the Postmodern Culture*[105] is the foundational underpinning for The Table and Children's Table ministry models and was authored by the founders of Creation Incubator. Creation Incubator was awarded a $1.25 million Lilly grant for the Christian Parenting and Caregiving Initiative to implement this model to benefit churches in a conference of the United Methodist Church. For more information about this ministry model, visit CreationIncubator.org/thetable.

[105] Kotan and Scott, *Inside Out* (Market Square Books) 2022.

CHAPTER FIVE

Relational Discipleship

We loved you so much that we shared with you
not only God's Good News but our own lives, too.

1 Thessalonians 2:8 (NLT)

We all want to be seen and known. We want to be "where everybody knows your name." How can this be fostered in a world that is insulated by cynicism, fear, and distrust? The church, to a large degree, has earned the distrust of seekers and the spiritually open. Building true, authentic relation*ships* is the only remedy. This involves trust. To build trust, you must be trustworthy over and over again.

In times past, the way to build the church and faith community was for a believer to invite their non-Christian friends to a revival meeting, a special church service, a Sunday-school guest event, or a youth event: "Come and see what we're doing." Today, this is rarely effective. On the rare occasions it does work, the guest is most likely dechurched or unhappy with their current church rather than a seeker or nonbeliever.

With the greater need for trust and relation*ship*-building, it is far more effective to say, "Tell me your story," or "Let's live life together." This won't be accomplished by "going to church" on Sunday, fulfilling an obligation. People are searching for community and a sense of belonging. Many have been ships without a port—drifting, hopeless, and alone.

We have erred in focusing solely on people being baptized or becoming members to "seal the deal." And too often, there have been no expectations beyond these sealing-the-deal actions for intentional disciple*ship* growth and accountability. Baptism and membership were the endgame—not the beginning of a disciple*ship* journey. Disciple*ship* is not a process that occurs by osmosis. Deepening disciple*ship* is a continuous process of transformation. If we truly believe that abundant, thriving life is in Jesus, then we must focus on moving people one step closer to a deeper relation*ship* with Jesus in everything we do, guiding them back—or closer—to the Lighthouse (Christ). How do we do that?

The Wesleyan Approach

John Wesley was deeply concerned about moving people toward a deeper relation*ship* with Jesus. He believed that conversion was only the beginning of the Christian journey. To help believers grow in grace and holiness (essential tenets of Wesleyan theology), he created a systematic method of spiritual formation rooted in structured, accountable community life, thereby founding the Methodist movement.

Wesley's disciple*ship* structure was both pastoral and missional, aimed at nurturing disciples who were growing in personal holiness and active in works of service.

Wesley organized his followers into a tiered system of small groups:

1. **Class Meetings.** These foundational small groups of ten to twelve people were designed to foster spiritual growth through mutual accountability, prayer, encouragement, and disciple*ship*. Attendees would regularly share about their spiritual lives, including struggles, temptations, victories, and areas of growth. Participation was not optional—regular attendance was expected and considered essential to one's spiritual (disciple*ship*) journey. While

they can be compared to modern small groups or cell groups, they placed a much stronger emphasis on accountability and intentional spiritual formation than today's typical Sunday school class or small group.

2. **Band Meetings.** Voluntary and more intimate by design, these groups aimed to foster deeper spiritual honesty and formation. Each consisted of just three to five people, typically grouped by gender and marital status. The focus was on confession, vulnerability, and mutual spiritual direction to help individuals confront specific personal sins, temptations, and spiritual blind spots in a safe and trusted environment. How many of these types of groups have you experienced or exist in your church?

3. **Societies.** Larger gatherings of believers, often functioning like today's local churches, were known as societies. Multiple class meetings would come together to form a society for worship, teaching, prayer, and singing. Unlike the more intimate, personal nature of classes and bands, societies offered a more public, corporate expression of the faith community. It is almost as if Wesley's methods were the reverse of today's common practices.

These deeply intentional, highly structured meetings helped people stay connected to God and one another in meaningful ways. This highly relational and intentional approach (relation*ship* and disciple*ship* together) resulted in the following outcomes:

- High levels of spiritual growth and accountability
- Strong lay leader*ship* development
- Deployment of disciples into communities, modeling the life of Christ

- Rapid spread of the (spiritual) movement, especially among the working class
- Empowerment of women and laypersons in ministry roles
- Transformation of communities through disciplined love-in-action

Tier	Focus	Size	Outcome
Class Meeting	Accountability, Encouragement	10 - 12	Ongoing spiritual growth and mutual care
Band Meeting	Confession, Deep Honesty	3 - 5	Inner transformation and holiness leading to entire sanctification
Society	Worship, Word, Community	100+	Spiritual formation in a corporate setting

Today, several denominations (e.g., United Methodist, Wesleyan, and Church of the Nazarene) still emphasize Wesley's disciple*ship* approach—though implementation varies. These churches often encourage small groups or "life groups" modeled after class meetings. They train lay leaders to lead these groups and focus on grace, holiness, and mission as key disciple*ship* outcomes.

In the digital age, methodical disciple*ship* is being adapted to online platforms. Apps and websites help people track spiritual practices, connect with accountability partners, and join online groups. Online versions of class meetings and band meetings can be offered through Zoom or group chats. And disciple*ship* platforms like Disciple*ship* Bands, developed by Seedbed,[106] offer digital tools for Wesleyan-style small groups.

---

106 Seedbed, https://seedbed.com/.

Churches today typically anticipate worship attendance as a first step, membership next, and then, hopefully, involvement in Sunday school or a small group. This seems almost backwards to the Wesleyan method. In today's church, there is typically no expectation, intentionality, or even accountability for a person's deepening disciple*ship*. While church leaders certainly desire deeper disciple*ship*, there are few consequences for those who remain passive spectators or quietly drift away from "port" altogether. Furthermore, for those churches that do offer classes, the main objective and outcome are typically to further congregants' head knowledge far more than to foster transformation—living life more and more like Jesus each day.

While methodical disciple*ship* is alive in some places, it faces some modern-day challenges. Many people resist the idea of accountability or confessing struggles to others. People worry that admitting failure, weakness, or struggle will make others think less of them—or even abandon or shame them. In many cultures, vulnerability is still wrongly equated with incompetence or fragility. When someone feels like they should be stronger, more successful, or more in control, confessing a struggle feels like admitting they've failed at being who they're "supposed" to be. Unfortunately, framing this vulnerability and accountability in terms of shame often leaves a person feeling that they are bad, not just that they did something bad. This is why having a safe, judgment-free, authentic harbor to be real with others in relation*ships* and in disciple*ship* is so extremely important—and much needed in today's culture. Social media has exacerbated this situation by saturating online spaces with the false perceptions of a joyous life full of rainbows and unicorns.

Another common reason why the methodical disciple*ship* model is challenging is that people may feel they don't have time for regular, intimate group meetings. Or they may trivialize the deep purpose of these small groups. In the digital age, we've grown comfortable with surface-level transparency, but we often shy away from the kind of raw vulnerability such groups engender. Could it be that people have not experienced this time of human connection and exchange to know the growth, understanding, and relation*ship*-building it can have?

Take a deeper look at Gen Z to better understand the struggles of engaging this generation in small groups. Generation Z (generally understood to be those born between 1995 and 2010) is often characterized by a paradox: a strong desire for meaningful relation*ships* alongside a reluctance to actively date or commit to traditional romantic partnerships. While a significant portion of Gen Z expresses interest in marriage and monogamous relation*ships*, surveys also reveal a high percentage remaining single and a general hesitation towards commitment.

People Coming Alongside One Another in Life

As Wesley's approach exemplifies, true disciple*ship* isn't just about passing on knowledge. It's about walking life's journey with someone, shoulder to shoulder, through the mess and meaning of life. It's about coming alongside others with humility, consistency, and love. A true spiritual mentor isn't a distant expert but a fellow traveler, someone who says, "I'm with you. Let's follow Jesus together." It's more than just walking a mile in someone's shoes; it's walking with them through their journey, side by side in shoes scuffed by shared roads, shared experiences, and shared stories.

This means living life in proximity, not just physical proximity—although virtual connections are not necessarily ineffective—but also emotional and spiritual closeness. It means showing up in weakness, not pretending to have it all together, but modeling what it looks like to struggle faithfully.

> *Be a human being first and an evangelist second.*
> *You will accomplish a lot more if you build a relationship*
> *with no ulterior motives by being open*
> *and listening to what they tell you.*[107]
>
> **Ryan Burge**

When a spiritual mentor or a fellow disciple hides their own struggles and weaknesses, they unintentionally create a false picture of the Christian life—one that suggests maturity equals perfection. But the Bible never paints such a picture. Even the apostle Paul spoke openly about his weaknesses, saying he would boast about them so that Christ's power might be displayed through him. By masking their humanity, mentors and fellow class members risk placing themselves as the model rather than pointing their disciples to Jesus, the only one truly worth imitating.

Authentic disciple*ship* is not about one person appearing strong while another learns to catch up. It's about walking together in grace. Vulnerability from a mentor or fellow disciple builds relational trust and gives the person being discipled permission to be honest about their own struggles. When a mentor says, "I've been there too, and here's how God met me," they offer hope and model what it means to depend on God's grace. Disciple*ship* that lacks honesty and transparency becomes performance-based, but when weakness is shared wisely and humbly, it creates a space for real transformation—not through perfection but through the ongoing presence and power of Christ.

Disciple*ship* is multi-dimensional, much like how people

---

[107] Burge, "Who Are the Nones?" *Leading Ideas.*

learn in different ways. Just as some people learn best through tactile experiences rather than lectures, spiritual growth also flourishes through relational, embodied, and experiential practices—not merely through information transfer. Sermons and Bible studies can be valuable, much like a lecture, but they often reach only the head. When we share our lives—our questions, struggles, doubts, and fears—we also engage the heart and soul of the disciple. Transforming disciple*ship* is what one feels, experiences, and lives with one another, not just hears. Transformation is action-oriented. Knowledge accumulation is often simply passive.

In the same way that hands-on learners need to do to understand, many believers grow most deeply when they walk alongside someone in real life, watching how faith is lived out rather than just explained. In fact, both people walking alongside one another experience growth! Sharing life becomes the spiritual equivalent of tactile learning: it moves formation from theory to transformation. It is disciple*ship* and relation*ship* together.

How is this lived out? Relational, everyday disciple*ship* looks like friend*ship* with spiritual intentionality. It happens in simple moments—like conversations over coffee or meals—where people share honestly about their hearts, their doubts, their struggles, and where they see God at work (or feel distant from God). It shows up in life-on-life moments, like running errands together or inviting someone into your home (and your life), where faith is modeled through how you handle stress, relation*ships*, and daily decisions.

Relation*ship*-based disciple*ship* also involves intentional check-ins throughout the week, demonstrating your commitment to walking alongside each other. It means making space for hard questions, responding with humility and curiosity rather than quick answers. And sometimes, it's as vulnerable as confessing sin, naming temptation, expressing doubts, and reminding one another of God's grace. Ultimately, this kind of disciple*ship* moves beyond programs or study guides; it's about doing ordinary life together in a way that helps each person become more like Jesus. It is disciple*ship* coupled with relation*ship.*

Seed that expresses the love and grace
and hope of Jesus Christ is never truly lost.
Don't give up!

Ryan P. Burge[108]

This relational disciple*ship* approach mirrors how Jesus discipled: He didn't just give his Sermon on the Mount; he also modeled it. He ate meals with others, took long walks with many different kinds of people, had hard conversations with his disciples and with strangers, and showed patient love to those with whom he lived life.

The Life of the Church Centers on Disciple*ship*

The church's sole purpose is disciple*ship.* The church exists to make disciples, not just to gather crowds. At its core, the church isn't a building or a weekly service. It's a community of people learning to live like Jesus, in relation*ship* with one another. And the central task Jesus gave his church wasn't to promote programs, pack pews, or perfect performances. It was to "Go and make disciples of all nations" (Matthew 28:19, NIV).

So, disciple*ship* isn't a part of church life—it is (or should be) the church's life. It's the heartbeat of everything the church is and does. Let's get practical. What does this type of relational

[108] Ryan P. Burge, *The Nones: Where They Came From, Who They Are, and Where They Are Going* (Minneapolis: Fortress Press, 2021).

discipleship look like in a local church?

1. **Every ministry is a disciple*ship* ministry.**

   Whether it's teaching kids, hosting a Bible study, or setting up chairs, each role should point people toward knowing, following, and becoming more like Christ. Hoping people figure out their discipleship journey on their own is replaced by leaving no doubts about the connection points for everything the church offers, including the weekly sermon. A church program may be fun, well-attended, and even meet a need in the community, but if it doesn't meet this "disciple*ship* test," perhaps another organization without the discipleship purpose should be providing these programs.

2. **Disciple*ship* is relational, not just instructional.**

   Jesus didn't just teach lessons—he shared life. Following Jesus' lead, the church must create space for deep relation*ships,* accountability, and mutual encouragement, not just for content or resource consumption. Disciple*ship* is transformational personally and collectively. Content consumption can be provided by any number of websites, podcasts, or streaming channels. Deep relation*ships* do not happen in these settings, as we established in Chapter 2.

3. **Worship, mission, and service all flow from disciple*ship*.**

   When people are growing as disciples:

   - Worship becomes more than music—it becomes a lifestyle.
   - Mission becomes natural—we share what's transforming us.
   - Service becomes joyful—we pour out what God is pouring in.

4. **Discipleship is the long game.**

   Relational discipleship is slow, messy, and deeply human. It's what Friedrich Nietzsche coined (and Eugene Peterson popularized) as a "Long obedience in the same direction." Churches centered on relational discipleship don't chase the new shiny thing; they invest in relationally driven formation that leads to transformation.

Imagine a church where the primary question isn't "How many attended?" but "Who's growing in Christ?" Imagine a church where people are known, not just counted, and where the goal is not just about program decisions but about transformation. That's what it looks like when the life of the church centers on disciple*ship* rooted in authentic relation*ships.*

Disciple*ship* Includes Evangelism

Evangelism is not separate from disciple*ship*—it's where disciple*ship* starts and continues to grow. Let's break this down:

In Matthew 4:19, Jesus says, "Follow me, and I will make you fishers of men." That simple yet profound invitation, "Follow me," serves as both a call to evangelism and the beginning of disciple*ship,* rooted in relation*ships,* to share the Good News with others. Jesus' approach didn't separate these two aspects of disciple*ship* and evangelism; he saw them as intertwined. Later, in the Great Commission (Matthew 28:19-20), Jesus didn't say, Get people saved and move on. Instead, he commanded, "Go and make disciples ... teaching them to obey everything I've commanded you." The process of making disciples starts with reaching people through building relation*ships,* demonstrating that evangelism naturally flows into, through, and out of disciple*ship.*

The winds of secularization and polarization are swirling like never before.

Most of that seed is going to fall on rocky soil, never to reap a harvest.

And it seems that there are fewer people to spread it every year. It's easy to give up hope.

But we must recall the words of the Apostle Paul to the church in Galatia:

"So let us not grow weary in doing what is right,

for we will reap at harvest time, if we do not give up."

Galatians 6:9 (NRSVUE)

Sharing the gospel without following up with relation*ship* and disciple*ship* can lead to shallow faith or even spiritual confusion. People may respond to the message emotionally but remain ill-equipped for a life of faith. They might believe, but without growth, their faith lacks depth, endurance, and the ongoing transformation of a life lived as an ever-growing disciple. As Jesus explains in the Parable of the Sower, the seed falling on "rocky ground" refers to someone who hears the word and at once receives it with joy. But since they have no spiritual roots, their journey lasts only a short time. When trouble or persecution comes, they quickly fall away (Matthew 13:20-21). This is why Jesus didn't call us merely to make converts but to make disciples—people who grow, mature, and are equipped to follow Jesus together daily.

A true disciple of Jesus doesn't remain focused only on personal growth. Rather, disciple*ship* always moves outward, toward others, embracing them (building loving relation*ships).* As people grow in Christ, they are shaped and transformed for mission (the Great Commission) and service (the Great Commandment). Evangelism becomes a natural outcome of a maturing relation*ship* with Jesus. When someone is truly walking with Jesus, they don't keep that relation*ship* hidden. Relational disciple*ship,* therefore, includes evangelism, because disciples replicate themselves by loving and reaching others. Maturing disciples have a profound desire to help others find a relation*ship* with Jesus, just as the disciples did, and to share the resulting love and transformation.

When disciples live out their faith authentically—marked by love, humility, and peace—it gives weight to their words and opens doors to meaningful relation*ships* and spiritual conversations. By investing in others in this way, a disciple's life becomes a powerful form of evangelism. Paul captured this when he said, "Follow me as I follow Christ" (1 Corinthians 11:1, NIV). The credibility of a transformed life, coupled with a love for others, draws others in and demonstrates the truth of the message we proclaim. Once again, there is a very clear understanding of how evangelism is steeped in the connection between relation*ship* and disciple*ship.*

Shaping Hearts in Childhood

Children should not be excluded from the privileges of growing in Christ. They, too, must have the opportunity to be discipled. Disciple*ship* for children is not a watered-down version of adult disciple*ship;* it's age-appropriate spiritual formation that meets kids where they are while calling them into a real, growing relation*ship* with Jesus. It's about teaching Bible stories, shaping hearts, habits, and identity in Christ.

It is never too early to begin discipling children. In fact, recent research confirms that children "learn what they live" and that one of the most critical windows for faith formation may be between birth and age three. When a child is born into a family that has a relation*ship* with God, the child is more likely to develop and experience an individual relation*ship* with God.

These important insights—and much more—are included in the National Study of Youth and Religion (NSYR).[109] How often do churches delay discipleship formation for children way beyond age three and miss the opportunities beginning as early as birth?

Rooted in Relation*ship*

Disciple*ship* for children, as with adults, begins and continues alongside relation*ships*. Kids are shaped more by people (particularly parents and caregivers, according to NSYR) than by programs. The most powerful spiritual formation happens through loving, consistent adults—such as parents, teachers, and mentors—who model Jesus in the rhythms of everyday life. Ask an adult who experienced transformational disciple*ship* as a child, and they will immediately point to a person rather than a program. A child may forget a Bible lesson, but they will remember being seen, loved, and listened to by someone who reflects Christ.

Scripture-Centered but Story-Shaped

Children absolutely need to hear the stories of Jesus, but they must be communicated in a way that reaches their imagination, not just their intellect. Jesus often taught through stories, questions, metaphors, and everyday examples—an ideal model for discipling kids. Just like with adults, stories help children engage emotionally and see how God's truth applies to their own lives. They need to hear, "You are part of what God is doing in the world," so they can find their place in God's larger story. This means that starting with the Book of Romans may not be the best idea.

---

[109] National Study of Youth and Religion, accessed November 15, 2025, https://youthandreligion.nd.edu/.

Modeled through Everyday Moments

According to Deuteronomy 6:6-7, God's commands are to be woven into daily life: "Talk about them when you sit at home and when you walk along the road." Disciple*ship* happens in car rides, during bedtime routines, in moments of conflict, and in celebrations. Each of these ordinary moments can become spiritual touchpoints. Ask guiding questions like, What does this moment teach us about Jesus? About love? About trust? How does Jesus teach us to treat others?

As ministry leaders, one of the most formative times we have had with children in our ministries was in the church van. In the cloistered holy space of the church van, while picking kids up for youth activities, taking them to and from summer camp, or mission trip travel, they share their fears, joys, hopes, and questions. These were sacred and formative disciple*ship* moments.

Practice and Participation

Children grow spiritually by doing, not just by listening. Disciple*ship* includes regular opportunities for kids to participate. Invite children to pray in their own words, to serve in meaningful ways, to participate in worship, to ask questions—and honor those questions—and to share their faith with siblings or friends. Growth happens when children are not just taught but entrusted with real roles in the life of faith.

Identity Formation

In a world full of noise, conflicting messages, and bullying, children need to hear one truth again and again: You are deeply loved by God. You are a child of God. You are made for good things in God's Kingdom.

Disciple*ship,* at its core, is helping a child understand who they are in light of who God is. When a child's identity is grounded in Christ, it shapes how they think, act, and live—not just now but for a lifetime.

Multi-Generational Disciple*ship:* Passing on Faith through Relation*ships* across Generations

The biblical narrative consistently highlights the importance of one generation investing in the next. In Deuteronomy 6:6-7, God instructs the people: "These commandments that I give you today are to be on your hearts. Impress them on your children. Talk about them when you sit at home and when you walk along the road, when you lie down, and when you get up" (NIV).

This vision of disciple*ship* is not academic—it is lived. It happens in everyday life, through consistent, intentional presence. The apostle Paul affirms this in 2 Timothy 1:5, where he acknowledges the generational transmission of faith from grandmother Lois to mother Eunice to grandson/son Timothy. Similarly, Titus 2 provides a framework for older men and women to teach and model the faith to younger people.

The vision of this rich mixture of relation*ship* and disciple*ship* is not rooted in a matriarch, patriarch, or imposed authoritarian leader*ship.* Servant leader*ship* is based on relational disciple*ship.* Relation*ship*-based disciple*ship* is defined as a church's focus on equipping and deploying disciples to serve, lead, and share in its port of call (the mission field or community the church is called to reach with the Good News of Christ).

A Model of Multi-Generational Disciple*ship*

Multi-generational disciple*ship* can be visualized as a relational chain of formation where each generation receives, lives out, and passes on the faith. This model includes four core generational roles:

1. **Legacy Generation (Elders, Grandparents, Seasoned Mentors)**

These wise guides share wisdom, tell stories of faith, and model spiritual perseverance. This generation brings the depth of life experience. They are called not to retire from ministry but to invest in the formation of younger believers. Their role is vital in offering perspective, encouragement, and stability. Their testimonies of God's faithfulness shape the imaginations and trust of the next generation.

Cross-mentoring is also very important. (Refer back to Chapter 2, where moms reported not feeling heard or seen.) Like the legacy generation invests in younger generations, mature disciples are open to continually learning and transforming through Christ. Hearing and learning from younger generations helps the legacy generation stay relevant and open to continuous learning. They do not hold on to power but help equip younger generations and hand over the reins of leader*ship.*

I (Kelly) have been blessed with five beautiful grandchildren. Since the first was born in 2012, I have kept a journal for each of them. I've shared my hopes and prayers for them, recounting the challenges their families have faced through the years and how God carried them through. I've also shared my own story of God's faithfulness, hoping to pass along the legacy of God's steadfast love that has deepened my own faith.

2. **Bridge Generation (Parents, Leaders, Adults in Mid-Life)**

Often in the busiest life stage, this group serves as a "bridge," simultaneously learning from mentors and mentoring others.

Their example at home, work, and in the church creates the context in which younger believers can see what mature faith looks like in practice. This generation anchors the model with their daily, relational investment in their children, aging parents, and the greater community.

3. **Emerging Generation (Teens and Young Adults)**

This generation is forming identity and discovering their call. Barna purports that 52 percent of Gen Zs are "very motivated" to know about Jesus.[110] They should not be sidelined or discounted but be welcomed into a holistic journey of disciple*ship*—learning, questioning, and serving. Emerging generations need a seat at the leader*ship* table so their voices can be heard, understood, and meaningfully shape ministry direction. As they mature, they should be empowered to take responsibility, including opportunities to mentor children and peers.

4. **Formative Generation (Children)**

Children must not be seen as the "church of tomorrow" but as disciples of Jesus today. Although we may not characterize it as disciple*ship,* the questions and observations of this age group about God, the Bible, and the world that are sometimes exhausting can be an opportunity for older Christ-followers to remember what it is like to have the faith of a child, reflect on their often deep insights, and study and research the biblical answers to their queries.

So, what are some practical ways to build a healthy multi-generational disciple*ship* culture? Intergenerational disciple*ship*

---

[110] "Most American Teens 'Very Motivated' to Know About Jesus: Barna," Christian Daily, accessed November 19, 2025, https://www.christiandaily.com/news/most-american-teens-very-motivated-to-know-about-jesus-barna.

thrives when structured around meaningful connection and relation*ship* with shared purpose. One powerful model is prayer partners, where each person is paired with someone older or someone younger. This creates a living chain of disciple*ship* that fosters growth, accountability, and continuity across generations. Rather than isolated instruction, disciple*ship* becomes a shared journey—everyone both gives and receives.

This kind of growth deepens through shared life and experiences. When generations spend time together in organic, life-giving ways—over meals, in acts of service, through honest conversations, and prayer—disciple*ship* becomes a natural part of everyday life. To support this, intentional rhythms such as wor*ship,* storytelling, and shared ministry help reinforce a sense of spiritual family. Importantly, reciprocal learning is at the heart of this model. While older generations offer wisdom and experience, younger ones bring fresh energy, new perspectives, and creative expressions of faith. True disciple*ship* isn't one-directional—it's mutual and transformative for all involved.

Strong weaving is required for a ship's fishing nets to be durable. The same is true for faith formation. An intricate weaving of discipleship and generational relation*ships* is key to formation across the ages.

Wrap-Up

Disciple*ship* is grounded in first being in relation*ship* with God and then others. For those who have no church experience, distrust churches and their leaders, or have been hurt by the church, the first step is to build trusting, authentic, nonjudgmental relation*ships* in the mission field with a Christ-follower. Gone are the days of throwing open the church doors and the community showing up. This attractional church model is all but gone. Unfortunately, too many churches still conduct ministry as if this approach is still true and effective. To live out the Great Commission (making disciples who transform the world) in our post-modern world, the church must rethink (with a sense of urgency) how it shows up and interacts with its community. This includes becoming relationally centered and deploying relationally grounded disciples—who have been equipped for a renewed movement—beyond the church walls.

Key Points

1. While the church is often seen as distrustful in surveys, building authentic relation*ships* is the foundation for disciple*ship* formation. Building relation*ships* with new people begins in the seas of life (the greater community or mission field), not in the port of call (the church facility).

2. Our faith and formation are rooted in the Wesleyan approach to disciple*ship,* which emerges from authentic, accountable relation*ships* and from investing in everyday life alongside one another.

3. Relation*ship*-based disciple*ship* is not solely intellectual learning. Rather, it is hearing, seeing, knowing, doing, transforming, and living life with one another as we continuously grow more Christlike.

4. Relation*ship*-based disciple*ship* isn't merely one of the ministries or programs a church offers. Relation*ship*-based disciple*ship* is the purpose of the church, the port of call. Everything, everyone, and all resources must drive and support the discipleship journey.

5. Evangelism is not separate from disciple*ship;* it is woven into the very fabric of becoming and being a disciple. Evangelism is the purest act of relation*ship*-based disciple*ship.*

6. Relation*ship*-based disciple*ship* is for all ages, from infancy to death. No one (including a disciple) is too young or too old for relation*ship*-based disciple*ship*.

7. Relation*ship*-based disciple*ship* is not intended to be age-segregated. Multi-generational relation*ship*-based disciple*ship* provides the intended practice of biblical formation.

Case Study

The Salvation Army Corps Community Center (Church) of Gwinnett County, Georgia, is intentionally breaking down generational barriers and mentoring youth through a unique prayer partner ministry. This ministry creates prayer-based partnerships between teens and adults within the church. These partnerships foster spiritual growth and meaningful connection across generations.

Open to students in sixth grade and above, the ministry offers the opportunity to be matched with a same-gender adult prayer partner. Church leader*ship* takes great care in the pairing process, thoughtfully matching partners based on the teen's unique needs and characteristics. After much prayer and discussion, spiritually mature adults with a strong track record of relation*ship*-based disciple*ship* and leader*ship* in the church are selected. Once the match is made and approved by the teen's parents or guardians, the adult is formally invited to step into a mentoring role in the student's spiritual journey.

To ensure a safe and supportive environment, full child safety protocols are in place at all times. These include certified adult mentors, monitored communication methods, active parental involvement, and all in-person interactions occurring in approved settings.

According to lay leader Jeremy Rowland, "The Prayer Partner Ministry has had great success in transforming the lives of our young people." He emphasizes that the goal is to encourage students toward spiritual growth, accountability, mentorship, and ultimately, Christlikeness. He adds, "The Prayer Partner Ministry will have an immeasurable impact on the student's life."

The ministry begins with a meet-and-greet breakfast, designed to build relation*ships* and foster an initial spiritual connection between the students and their adult partners. This is followed by a dedication ceremony during a Sunday worship service, officially recognizing and commissioning the prayer partner*ships*. Throughout the year, quarterly prayer moments are incorporated into worship services to sustain and celebrate the spiritual journey of each pair. Looking ahead, the church also plans to host joint service projects, including a day of ministry where prayer partners will serve side-by-side in future ministry activities.[111]

[111] "Disciple: Intergenerational Prayer in Action," The Salvation Army USA, accessed November 15, 2025, https://www.salvationarmyusa.org/stories/disciple-intergenerational-prayer-in-action/.

CHAPTER SIX

Discipleship for the Orbital Port

Take the things you heard me say
in front of many other witnesses
and pass them on to faithful people
who are also capable of teaching others.

2 Timothy 2:2 (CEB)

If a new follower of Jesus became engaged in your congregation today, what pathway would you offer them to grow as a disciple? What intentional steps, experiences, beliefs, and actions would this journey include? How do more mature disciples journey alongside new believers? What ministries and programs are in place that intentionally help disciples mature?

How does a church know if there is development and growth in its existing disciples? Being a member of a small group or a Sunday school class does not necessarily equate to disciple*ship* development. I (Kay) have found multiple situations in which these gatherings focused more on social connections or on caring for one another. There is nothing wrong with this focus, yet let's be clear that this is disciple*ship* development. In other situations, the focus of gatherings is mostly on gaining intellectual understanding or knowing the stories in the Bible. Again, there is absolutely nothing wrong with this focus, but we must understand that this is only part of developing disciples. Obtaining information and understanding without transformation is only a partial disciple*ship* pathway.

Jesus came near and spoke to them,
"I've received all authority in heaven and on earth.
Therefore, go and make disciples of all nations,
baptizing them in the name of the Father and of the Son and of the Holy Spirit,
teaching them to obey everything that I've commanded you.
Look, I myself will be with you every day until the end of this present age."

Matthew 28:18-20 (CEB)

The instructions Jesus gave are very clear. He sent his disciples to teach all that they had learned from him, resulting in more disciples. Dear readers, this is THE purpose for each and every church. Yet, too often, churches have a haphazard approach to growing and developing disciples at best, and church leaders have grown frustrated with the congregants' lack of commitment, engagement, and focus. There is a direct correlation between deficient intentional disciple*ship* development and congregational disconnection.

In my (Kay's) consulting work, I find that most churches have no disciple*ship* pathway whatsoever. And for those who have a disciple*ship* pathway, it is either not used or is this "thing" that exists, but nothing aligns with it or points people to engaging with it. Sometimes the pathway was created by a pastor, and when that pastor left, the disciple*ship* pathway was shelved. The congregation was not committed to the pathway as a needed and valued source of disciple*ship* development.

A disciple*ship* pathway is sometimes treated as a program rather than a tool central to developing and growing disciples. Sometimes a committee creates a church's disciple*ship* pathway as an appointed task. The committee faithfully completes the task, but the pathway is never truly launched or communicated well, and it lacks the ministries, resources, and focus allocated to its adoption or implementation.

A discipleship pathway is typically a narrated journey that identifies development steps for a disciple. Often, churches offer a visual representation of the pathway to help disciples more clearly understand. While the narration and the pathway graphic may appear sequential, a disciple's journey is typically not sequential. It is the shifting momentum—forward and backward—that shapes their journey.

The Discipleship Pathway

Let's take a look at the elements a discipleship pathway might include. The following chart is used in the Catalyst Initiative of the Baltimore-Washington Conference of the United Methodist Church.[112] The chart, adapted from the work of Phil Maynard[113] and the United Methodist Rule of Discipleship,[114] provides definitions of discipleship that include the actions of disciples in the marketplace and developmental markers ranging from exploring to maturing. This chart describes the discipleship journey from a Wesleyan perspective. Churches can use this to help define their discipleship pathway. It can be used as a stand-alone measurement when an assessment is created to help track or measure people's growth and movement within the various elements of the pathway.

Discipleship isn't a destination—it's a holistic journey of grace.

---

[112] Baltimore-Washington Conference of The United Methodist Church, Catalyst Initiative, accessed November 19, 2025, https://www.bwcumc.org/article/catalyst-initiative/.

[113] Phil Maynard and Eddie Pipkin, Discipler: *An Interactive Guide to Intentional, Relational, Accountable Discipleship* (Nashville: United Methodist Discipleship Ministries/EMC^3, 2017).

[114] The United Methodist Church, *The Book of Discipline of The United Methodist Church* 2020/2024 (Nashville: United Methodist Publishing House, 2024), ¶1117.2.

Column 1: Everywhere we go, we can choose to act like followers of Jesus or not. In the far-left column are the actions of disciples in the marketplace. Missing any one of these actions is to miss an aspect of what it means to love like Jesus.

Column 2: These aspects of disciple*ship* come from the rule of disciple*ship* and loving like Jesus loves.

Columns 3-6: Each square within the column describes how a person might describe themselves for each aspect of disciple*ship* from the rule of disciple*ship*.

1	2	3	4	5	6
Actions of Disciples in the Marketplace	RULE OF DISCIPLE*SHIP*	EXPLORING	BEGINNING	GROWING	MATURING
Demonstrates radical hospitality and shares faith as led by the Holy Spirit.	INCLUSIVE WITNESS	I am drawn to Christians who graciously accept me as if I belong with them already.	I am called not only to receive, but also to offer God's gracious acceptance and invitation to others, including those who are different from me.	I seek to both relate and adapt how I approach others—both in the church and the world—to reflect God's hospitality toward me and the wide diversity of people God has created.	To share God's love, I intentionally seek to build relation*ships* with people inside and outside my culture and faith tradition.
Helps out no matter the position or role and invites others to serve in alignment with their interests.	COMPASSION-ATE SERVICE	I am often amazed at the way some disciples selflessly serve others to meet immediate needs, and I want to make a difference as well.	I know Christ invites me to join him in serving with those who are most vulnerable, and I'm discovering how God has gifted me to do this.	I experiment by serving in different areas across lines of difference so that I can discover how God might want to use my gifts, talents, and passions (to make whole what needs healing).	I join Jesus in mission among the most vulnerable, using my God-given gifts, talents, and passions, and help others discover where they may be called to serve.

Practices behaviors of inclusion, diversity, equity, and antiracism.	PERSISTENT JUSTICE	I join friends in marches or letter-writing campaigns if it is convenient or I feel a need.	I know that as I grow in my personal faith, I also need to work more consistently for justice and peace in my community, and I am open to learning the causes of suffering for those on the margins of my community.	I work with others to name the root causes of pain and suffering that people who live at the margins of society endure.	I join Jesus and others to repair broken systems and structures that oppress, marginalize, and devalue God's people and God's creation, and I engage in this sacred work as a means of grace.
Recognizes the image of God in the other and expresses reverence and worthiness of that child of God in each encounter.	WHOLE-HEARTED WORSHIP	I attend worship when a friend invites me, it is convenient, or I feel a need. I may give some when I attend worship.	I attend worship regularly, but I am growing to realize that I must attend to God every day. I am giving more and more regularly.	I attend worship regularly and set aside time daily for personal worship. I am tithing 10%, and I am considering how I am spending the other 90%.	I honor God in the ways I work, plan, and engage others in relation*ships*. I am tithing and consciously reordering my life to free up more resources to honor God and bless others.
Offers a word of encouragement authentically and humbly, rooted in God's great love, mercy, and grace without being "churchy" or judgmental. Offers prayer as led by the Holy Spirit.	MINDFUL DEVOTION	I am drawn to the story of God's love and am beginning to explore the scriptures for myself and through Bible studies with others.	I am developing a daily practice of prayer, scripture, and devotional reading, opening myself to God, and am committed to becoming more like Jesus.	I am exploring new spiritual disciplines and experiencing a greater level of intimacy with God as I daily seek to apply the teachings of Jesus to my own life.	I am taking responsibility for my own growth through the daily practice of spiritual disciplines and partnering with God to help others grow in openness and obedience to Christ.

Stages of the Disciple*ship* Journey

Yet another disciple*ship* pathway option is the one below, adapted from The Critical Journey by Janet Hagberg and Robert Guelich.[115]

---

[115] Janet O. Hagberg and Robert A. Guelich, *The Critical Journey: Stages in the Life of Faith*, 2nd ed. (Salem, WI: Sheffield Publishing, 2005).

STAGES OF FAITH	CHARACTERISTICS	HOW WE GET CAGED	HOW WE MOVE TO THE NEXT STAGE
STAGE ONE recognition of God "we believe"	A sense of awe & need for a savior and greater meaning in life. A sense of innocence & openness.	If we stick to a sense of whiteness and ignorance and don't believe we are really worth "more".	Become part of a strong group; take on more significance; follow a charismatic leader that provides direction.
STAGE TWO life of discipleship "we are learning about God"	Meaning comes from belonging; answers found in a leader, cause or belief system; security in our faith.	Becoming rigid in righteousness, rule-following, or a "we against them" attitude.	Recognize uniqueness, identify giftedness, and what we contribute to the community.
STAGE THREE the productive life "we are about doing things for God"	Belonging in community, responsibility, active participation in work, home, and church.	Overzealousness, weariness in doing good, performance-based faith.	Loss of certainty, faith crisis, seeking guidance and direction.
THE WALL "Things just aren't working anymore... there's got to be more"			
STAGE FOUR the journey inward "we need to figure out a new way to do this relationship with God & others	Faith crisis, loss of certainty, search for direction rather than answers.	Over-questioning, immobilization, constant self-assessment.	Surrender, healing, forgiveness, reflection, discernment.
STAGE FIVE the journey outward "learning to live out of a totally different place"	Renewed calling, deep relationships, calm, focus on others.	Seen by others as impractical or unconcerned with urgency	Not striving; growing deeper; seeing God in all of life.
STAGE SIX the life of love "It's all about God"	Obedient, compassionate living, detachment from stress and possessions.	Seen as detached from the world or wasting life.	

Again, this disciple*ship* pathway can be used to identify the various concentric circles in the orbital model or as a standalone tool if an assessment is created to measure how individuals enter the pathway, advance through it, and grow into subsequent stages.

The Orbit Model

I planted, Apollos watered, but God made it grow.
Because of this, neither the one who plants
nor the one who waters is anything,
but the only one who is anything is God who makes it grow.
The one who plants and the one who waters work together,
but each one will receive their own
reward for their own labor.
We are God's coworkers, and you are
God's field, God's building.

1 Corinthians 3:6-9 (CEB)

As you develop your church's disciple*ship* pathway, consider how it intersects with your church's mission (making disciples who transform the world) and the desired movement (growth in disciple*ship* and leader*ship).* As always, we also have a responsibility to go and share the Good News with others as part of being a disciple and a faith community. This means that more people will come to know Christ.

Let's take a look at disciple*ship* from the perspective of an orbit. At the center of these concentric circles is Jesus. Jesus is the "bull's-eye." Think of this graphic as a representative of your personal orbit and the church's orbit. The idea is to identify and monitor the total number of people in the church's orbit and how people are taking steps into a deeper relation*ship* with Jesus. As part of disciple*ship,* we are to be disciple-makers.

Therefore, each disciple also has an orbital influence.

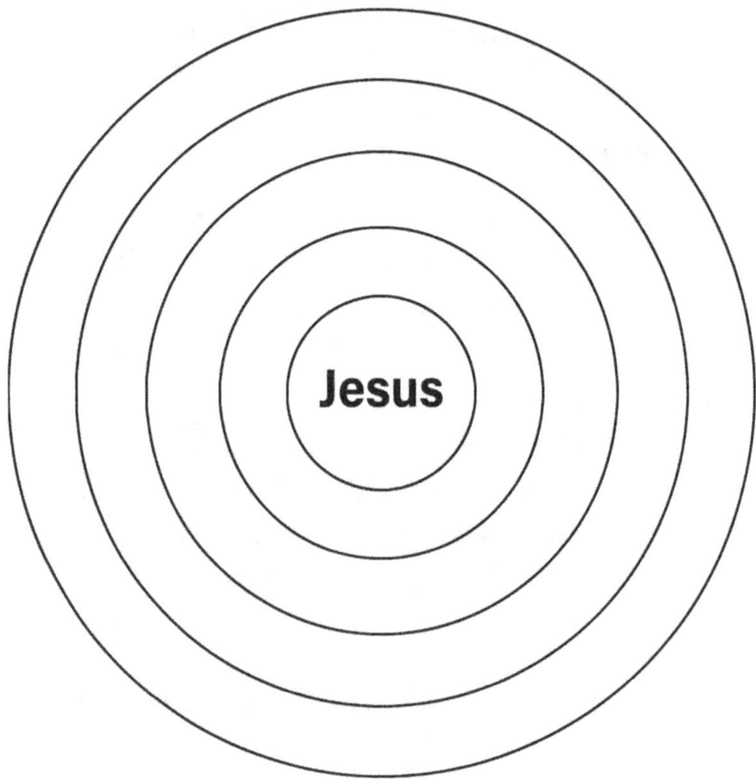

The whole orbital concept is centered on the three piers of becoming an orbital port (church): relation*ships*, disciple*ship*, and leader*ship*. This includes building new relation*ships*, deepening relation*ships* with one another, being in relation*ships* where faith-sharing can occur, serving together as Christ demonstrated, being in an ever-growing relation*ship* with Christ, helping others grow in their relation*ship* with Christ (disciple*ship*), and leading others to help build relation*ships* (leader*ship*).

The graphic below depicts a more developed orbit. You'll notice a variety of people in the various stages of both disciple*ship* and relation*ship* development. Note, a more mature disciple may be represented in the inner circles of the orbit related to their personal disciple*ship* journey but may also be represented in the outer circles of the orbit in their leader*ship* (leading ministries in fringe-serving and relation*ship*-building), relation*ship* (building relation*ships* with new people in the greater community), and disciple*ship* (becoming a disciple-maker who is transforming the world) development.

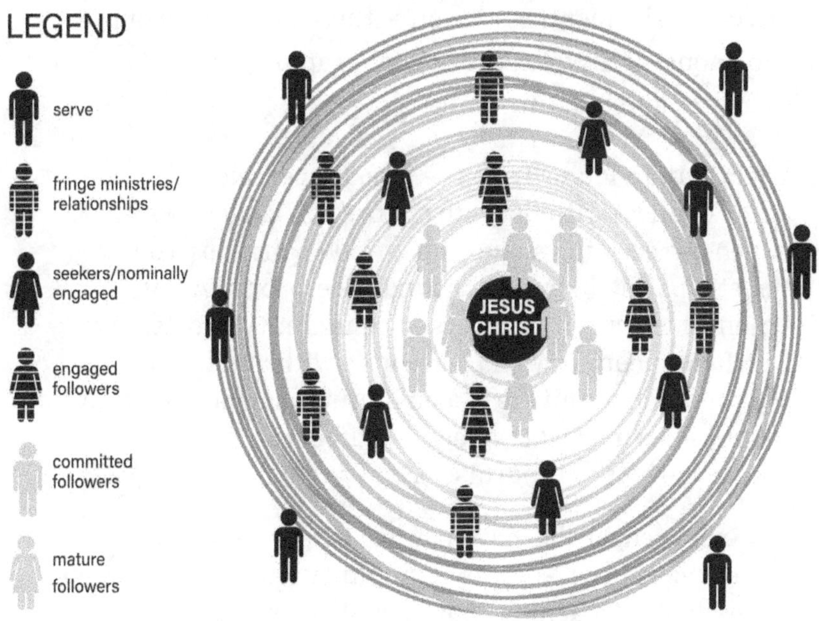

Notice the six unique development stages indicated on the graphic above, from "serve" to "mature followers." Your church may very well decide to create different names for the various stages or even identify more or fewer stages as you create your church's orbit.

We offer the orbit concept as a visual and a tool to help church leaders think about the development of new relation*ships*, disciples, and leaders as a holistic, relational development approach rather than three totally separate strategies or pathways. All these relational development journeys are concentric; all the steps in relation*ship*-building, the disciple*ship* journey, and leader*ship* development are interrelated and concentric. A church's disciple*ship* pathway is represented in the church's orbit, as is the development of new relation*ships* and leader*ship*.

Again, your church may decide to use different terms and stages of development, but we offer these definitions of the development stages from the orbital graphic provided earlier in this chapter as a starting point:

- Serve: Individuals from the broader community who connect with the church through various ways, such as receiving support (e.g., food pantry patrons), participating in events or fundraisers, or serving alongside church members in community efforts. This includes people the church serves with and in the greater community (e.g., community members who serve alongside church attenders, neighbors who attend a church event or fundraiser).

- Fringe: People who have new or distant relation*ships* with the church, such as community partners, a church's preschool or learning center, facility tenants, support groups, community groups, or scouting groups who use the church facility.

- Seekers: People who are intentionally seeking a relation*ship* with a spiritual community and/or God, or those who are nominally involved in the life of the church.

- Engaged: Those who are regularly involved in the life of the church and its mission field.

- Committed: People who are intentionally developing as disciples and are growing in their relation*ship* with Jesus Christ through consistent prayers, presence, gifts, service, and witness.
- Mature: People who have a deep relation*ship* with Jesus Christ, are deeply committed to fulfilling the Great Commandment and the Great Commission, and are committed to Kingdom impact and others coming to know Christ.

The believers devoted themselves to the apostles' teaching, to the community, to their shared meals, and to their prayers.
A sense of awe came over everyone.
God performed many wonders and signs through the apostles.
All the believers were united and shared everything.
They would sell pieces of property and possessions
and distribute the proceeds to everyone who needed them.
Every day, they met together in the temple and ate in their homes.
They shared food with gladness and simplicity.
They praised God and demonstrated God's goodness to everyone.
The Lord added daily to the community those who were being saved.

Acts 2:42-47 (CEB)

As your church considers the various stages of development of the people in its orbit, you will also want to consider what the concentric circles represent within your church's orbit. Again, consider these circles as the development stages of relation*ships*, disciple*ship*, and leader*ship*.

In the sample below, we have used a very simple pathway that starts with building new relation*ships* in your community or with those on the fringes of the church. Don't forget to note the mission field, which is represented by all the white space surrounding your orbit. The next circle inside the new relation*ships* might represent the ways people serve both inside and outside the church. Notice how each inner concentric circle is a progressive step in growing disciples, becoming more Christlike, and a deepening relation*ship* with Christ. Repeat the process to identify the development steps for disciple*ship* and leader*ship*. You may find overlap among the three development pathways of relation*ships*, disciple*ship*, and leader*ship*. That's okay. In fact, it is probably a good indicator that alignment and focus are becoming clearer.

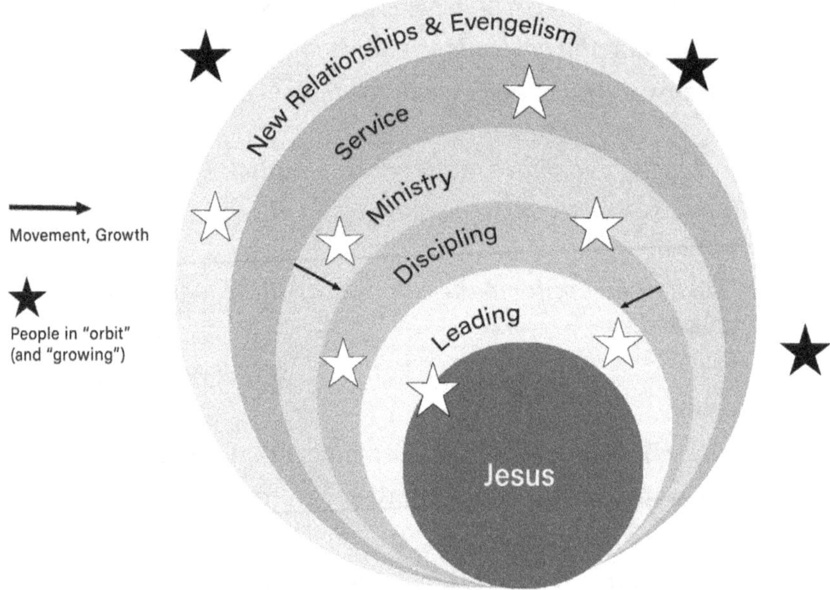

The orbital graphic is designed to identify logical, intentional steps for growing disciples, leaders, and relation*ships*. It also helps us identify if and how people are moving in or out of your orbit. Of course, the idea is to help people grow deeper into the orbit towards Christ. If people are moving outward in your orbit or even leaving it, you know changes are needed. The hope is that you have people developed at the deepest levels of your orbit who also move out to the mission field and the outer limits of your orbit, walking alongside others as they enter and navigate the orbit by building new relation*ships*, serving, and so on.

In considering the orbital model, you will likely need to shift the current culture regarding leader*ship* and equipping leaders. In the orbital model, leaders will focus on helping those they lead in their ministry area take their next step in the disciple*ship* journey. This focus may be quite different from a ministry team leader's current leader*ship* approach. Oftentimes, ministry team leaders concentrate more on accomplishing the tasks of their ministry area and on maintaining their team. In the orbital model, ministry team leaders focus on developing their team members to potentially step out or beyond that ministry area as part of their growth and disciple*ship* or leader*ship* journey.

Designing and implementing an orbital ministry model will take time, attention, focus, and likely a shift in ministry culture. All the elements of any ministry will be based on your church's orbit and development through the concentric circles of relation*ships,* disciple*ship,* and leader*ship.* This approach will challenge ministry silos, traditional methods of ministry, and compartmentalization. The orbital model offers a simple, holistic, and focused approach to the relational ministry of growing disciples.

The orbit approach is offered as a way to effectively refocus the church's resources to increase the number of relation*ships* it is building and deepen relation*ships* with Christ. Instead of launching programs or tweaking Sunday mornings with the hope of getting people to participate, the orbital approach helps us focus more on building relation*ships,* disciple*ship,* and leader*ship* for greater impact, transformation, and becoming more Christlike. In other words, the orbital approach shifts churches from focusing on the strategy to first focusing on developing relation*ships!*

A healthy, vital church increases the number of people within its orbit and helps them take their next step in the orbit of relation*ships,* disciple*ship,* and leader*ship.* Such churches create a clear pathway for relational growth with one another and with Christ. Their orbit provides clarity, momentum, energy, and alignment with its orbit. A healthy, vital church helps its people develop personal orbits grounded in disciple*ship,* relation*ships,* and leader*ship.* Identifying your church's orbit allows a simple approach to measuring missional effectiveness and the health of your church.

Connecting Disciple*ship,* Relation*ships,* and Leader*ship*

We must move away from a programmatic, Sunday-centric approach for the growth and development of disciples. Rather than starting with program development, healthy and vital churches understand that reaching more people and helping them grow deeper in their relation*ship* with Jesus Christ are what truly matter. Rather than investing the majority of church resources (time, dollars, energy, focus) in the Sunday morning experience, healthy, vital churches concentrate more on growing new relation*ships* and helping people grow in their relation*ship* with Christ (disciple*ship* and leader*ship*), resulting in the transformation of the people and their communities.

People who call your mission field home

People in your mission field who have a touch point with your church

People regularly involved in the life of the church

People who have a growing relationship with Christ

People deeply committed to walk with Christ and introducing others to Jesus

Take a look at the funnel above. It represents a process for building new relation*ships* and fostering disciple*ship* growth. The widest part of the funnel signifies the people who call your mission field home (e.g., neighborhood, town, or city you are called to reach). As the funnel narrows, it denotes the people in your mission field who have a point of contact with your church (e.g., a food pantry or a guest at an event). Further down the funnel are those who are regularly involved in the life of the church (e.g., worship attenders or small-group participants). As the funnel narrows even more, you'll find those who have a growing relation*ship* with Christ (disciple*ship)* and are serving the church in some way. At the very narrowest part of the funnel, one would find those who are deeply committed to walking through life with Christ, introducing others to Jesus, and helping them on their disciple*ship* journey. Oftentimes, these people are leaders of the church.

> *I am the vine; you are the branches. If you remain in me and I in you, you will bear much fruit; apart from me you can do nothing. If you do not remain in me, you are like a branch that is thrown away and withers; such branches are picked up, thrown into the fire and burned. If you remain in me and my words remain in you, ask whatever you wish, and it will be done for you. This is to my Father's glory, that you bear much fruit, showing yourselves to be my disciples.*
>
> **John 15:5-8 (NIV)**

Wrap-Up

When a stone is thrown into the water, it displaces the water and creates waves and ripples. Likewise, when a ship moves in the water, it also displaces the water and creates waves. Movement, decisions, and choices in an individual's life and the life of the church cause waves and ripples. The effect of these movements, decisions, and choices have a ripple effect. Think of this ripple effect as the resulting orbit for individual ships (people) and for the port (church).

Without a clear understanding and a pathway for developing disciples, a church will continue to flounder regardless of how large its attendance is. Disciple*ship* development tends to the very purpose of the church. Without it, the purpose becomes unfocused and often reverts to pleasing people and keeping them comfortable. That's not at all the intention Jesus had in mind when he shared the Great Commission. The disciple*ship* pathway lays the very foundation for the church's ministry. Without it, a church is built on the proverbial shifting sand.

Key Points

1. Develop a disciple*ship* pathway to clearly articulate and guide disciples in their discipleship journey.
2. It is more important to have a discipleship pathway than to spend years developing the "perfect" one.
3. Having a clearly defined and aligned discipleship pathway helps the church become more missionally aligned and focused.
4. Develop overlapping pathways for the development of relation*ships*, discipleship, and leadership that become the focus and driver for all decisions and resource allocation, and have associated vitality markers for each.
5. Focused, intentional church systems need to be in place to facilitate the desired missional outcomes, such as a discipleship pathway, a leadership development process, and intentional methods for building relation*ships*.
6. Focused and intentional ministries need to be in place to drive the desired missional outcomes, such as an evangelism team, a leadership development team (this is the nominations committee in the United Methodist Church and the Pastoral Care Committee in The Salvation Army), and a discipleship team that points disciples to the discipleship pathway and coordinates ministries and growth opportunities to support and grow disciples.

Case Study

Maria came to The Salvation Army through the Pathway of Hope program. She was a single mother of two, struggling with housing instability and underemployment. At first, her relation*ship* with The Salvation Army was primarily about meeting urgent needs—food assistance, rental support, and coaching to set small, achievable goals.

The corps officer (pastor) and case manager realized that while Maria was receiving support, the broader ministry teams often viewed their role as simply "providing services." The emphasis was on completing tasks—running the pantry, processing applications, or staffing the children's program. What was missing was the intentional focus on helping people like Maria take their next step in disciple*ship* and leader*ship*.

The corps began to apply the orbital model:

- **Relation*ships*:** Maria was intentionally connected to the women's ministry team, not just as a recipient of help but as someone with gifts to share. A team leader took the time to get to know her story, pray with her, and invite her to join a small-group Bible study.
- **Disciple*ship*:** Rather than only asking Maria to attend programs, the leader asked questions about her faith journey: "Where do you see God at work in your life right now?" and "What step do you want to take to grow closer to Christ?" Maria began to see herself as a disciple on a journey rather than a client.
- **Leader*ship*:** Over time, Maria expressed interest in serving at the pantry where she once received food. The ministry leader encouraged her, helped her build confidence, and gave her opportunities to take on responsibilities. Eventually, Maria was not only volunteering but also mentoring new clients, sharing her story of hope.

This journey meant that Maria secured stable employment and housing, completing her Pathway of Hope goals. Spiritually, she moved from being a recipient of ministry to an active disciple and leader within the corps. Her children became engaged in youth programs, growing up in a church orbit centered on relation*ships*, disciple*ship*, and leader*ship*. And the ministry team shifted from a task-centered mindset to a developmental, relational approach, asking not just "What needs to get done?" but "How is this helping someone take the next step in their disciple*ship* and leader*ship* journey?"

Maria's story illustrates how the orbital model reframes ministry. Instead of siloed tasks or program maintenance, leaders intentionally cultivated relation*ships*, disciple*ship*, and leader*ship*. The result was not only Maria's transformation but also the transformation of the corps (church) culture itself—becoming a healthy, vital church with momentum, clarity, and energy in its orbit.

CHAPTER SEVEN

Leader*ship* for the Orbital Port

As a church leader, it is often difficult to navigate shifting winds, high tides, and the challenges of an aging shipping fleet. There is often tension between the desire to return to the heyday of yesterday and the changes required by the church if it is to become (or remain) missionally effective. While the port of call (church) remains the preferred option for those remaining, there is an increasing disconnect from new *ships* docking at the pier. New *ships* are searching for community, meaning, and impact. The aging shipping fleet at the port is often most focused on staying afloat and ensuring its safety: safety from the steep learning curves associated with new engine technology, safety from voyaging out into the unknown deep seas that once called them, safety from the discomfort of leaving the port, and safety from risking the loss of any of the ships in their fleet by making changes or creating any discomfort.

Those who sign on and depart the system of anxious scarcity become the historymakers in the neighborhood.

Walter Brueggemann[116]

Leaders can easily find their church unknowingly or unintentionally dry-docked. When a ship becomes dry-docked, it is removed from the water and taken out of service. Ships can be in dry dock for weeks or months, depending on the extent of

[116] Walter Brueggemann, Journey to the Common Good (Louisville, KY: Westminster John Knox Press, 2010).

work required. Typically, the purpose of dry-docking a ship is to clean it, paint it, perform major repairs, complete renovations, or install upgrades and innovations. Churches can be dry-docked, too, for a variety of reasons. Those reasons include intentional and intensive training and teaching for deployment. However, they are often in danger of becoming permanently dry-docked through fear, a scarcity mindset, being overly focused on those already gathered, turning a blind eye to their mission field, becoming culturally irrelevant, losing capacity for ministry implementation, conflict, distrust, and a lack of leader*ship.*

In a relation*ship*-based disciple*ship* model, ministry leader*ship* is not a collection of experts or scholars. Rather, ministry leaders are continuously adapting, learning, relearning, and unlearning. They are flexible, humble, adaptable, and accountable servant leaders. In this relation*ship*-based disciple*ship* model, ministry leader*ship* walks alongside to support, encourage, mentor, teach, and ultimately deploy disciples.

Board Leader*ship* at the Port of Call

The port of call (church) desiring to become or remain a preferred port of call requires leader*ship* to be diligently focused on its missional call. In our nautical metaphor, think of the leader*ship* board as the port authority. In a port of call, the port authority works with other agencies, the business community, and stakeholders to coordinate efforts and achieve their port's goals. In the same way, a local church's leader*ship* board strategically plans and aligns resources to achieve missional fruitfulness and Kingdom impact.

A port without wise leader*ship* becomes a place of chaos. It takes steady vision to guide arrivals and departures into harmony and shared purpose. In a port, leader*ship* is the unseen tide that orders comings and goings; without it, the harbor becomes a hazard. A port of call thrives not by the number of ships it welcomes but by the wisdom that organizes its purpose. Without purpose (mission), there may be countless ships welcomed never to return. Leader*ship* in the harbor transforms traffic into teamwork and arrivals into opportunities.

IN A PORT OF CALL

A port without wise leadership becomes a place of chaos; it takes steady vision to guide arrivals and departures into harmony and shared purpose

Leader*ship* in a port of call (the leader*ship* board) is responsible for resource and missional alignment. A port without alignment may welcome many ships, but with no shared mission, the harbor becomes only a holding place, not a launching point. When port leader*ship* aligns with mission, every arrival strengthens the whole, and every departure carries the vision farther. Missional alignment in a port of call is the difference between random traffic and purposeful movement. A harbor with aligned leader*ship* is more than safe waters; it becomes a sending place of direction, destiny, and shared calling. Without missional alignment, even a busy port drifts into chaos; with it, each ship finds its place in the greater journey.

The Pastoral Leader*ship* at the Port of Call

The port of call (church) desiring to become or remain a preferred port of call requires particular types of leader*ship* skills and passions. In our nautical metaphor, think of the pastor as the escort tugboat. A pastor (escort tugboat) guides people (ships) into the harbor (church) for rest, renewal, and alignment, and then escorts them back out to sea (the mission field) for Kingdom impact.

Unlike the majestic ship or the bustling port, an escort tugboat's purpose is quiet but critical: guiding, escorting, and ensuring safe passage. A tugboat isn't the largest vessel, but it packs remarkable strength for its size. Likewise, a pastor doesn't carry the cargo (the people's lives or ministries) but uses spiritual strength to guide them safely. The escort tugboat doesn't overshadow the ship; it empowers it to arrive and depart safely. So too, a pastor quietly provides the strength of guidance to keep the church aligned for Kingdom impact.

Tugboats help ships enter and exit harbors that are too narrow, shallow, or complex for them to maneuver alone. A pastor helps people navigate transitions, crises, and seasons of change when trying to steer alone could leave them adrift or even cause real damage. Just as a tugboat knows the hidden channels of a harbor, a pastor helps people discern God's safe passage through life's unseen currents.

Tugboats are essential for movement—not just arrival. They ensure the ship is not stuck in the harbor (or stuck out to sea) and can leave again on its mission. A pastor helps the congregation re-engage in mission for the Kingdom, not remain docked in comfort. The escort tugboat pastor does not let the ship remain safely anchored; they nudge it out into the deep where the Kingdom calls.

Tugboats operate behind the scenes. Passengers on the ship may hardly notice them. Pastoral leader*ship* is often unnoticed, but its impact can be enormous. The tugboat's strength is measured not in visibility but in the ships it sets free to sail. Pastors, likewise, find purpose in unseen service for the Kingdom's advance.

Ministry Leader*ship* at the Port of Call

The port of call (church) desiring to become or remain a preferred port of call requires ministry leader*ship* (paid and unpaid ministry team leaders) to think of themselves as harbor stewards. Harbor stewards are the hands-on link between ships and the port, ensuring that what arrives at the port reaches its next destination safely. Their purpose is to ensure ships are efficiently serviced, loaded, and unloaded so vessels can continue their journeys safely and on schedule.

When ships arrive and depart, harbor stewards handle mooring lines, guide vessels into berths, and prepare for loading and unloading. While ships are docked, they move cargo in and out of the ship, often on tight schedules, and ensure customs and security protocols are followed. Harbor stewards assist with problem-solving, such as cargo shifts, equipment failures, and weather disruptions. They coordinate logistics to track the movement of the ship's cargo and support ships by assisting with refueling, waste disposal, and resupplying the ship's essentials. These well-equipped harbor stewards step in to provide emergency intervention in the event of spills, safety hazards, or urgent repair needs, minimizing risks and delays.

Let's examine the connection between the harbor steward and a ministry team leader. In addition, we will provide a translation of the vital role of the harbor steward to the vital role of a ministry team leader.

Harbor Steward	**Ministry Team Leader**
Mooring lines and ship guidance	Connecting people and programs to the disciple*ship* pathway via ministries
Loading and unloading cargo	Helping people identify their gifts and talents while shedding personal untruths
Scheduling and coordination	Scheduling events, coordinating people, and ensuring alignment of all to the ministry's objectives and ultimately the mission
Custom and security protocols	Ensuring all processes and procedures are known and followed
Intervention	Missional accountability
Track the movement of cargo	Develop disciples and track their growth in relation*ships,* discliple*ship,* and leader*ship*
Repairs and safety hazards	Course correct as needed to remain missionally aligned and effective
Equipment failures, weather disruptions	Be adaptable, flexible, and innovative while remaining on course with the mission
Refuel and resupply essentials	Identify, recruit, equip, and deploy disciples for ministry, missional fruitfulness, and Kingdom impact

In the orbital port model, the focus for ministry leader*ship* (e.g., ministry team leaders, paid staff) shifts from the traditional roles these leaders have fulfilled in the past. Unfortunately, the outdated model of ministry leader*ship* has too often produced passive pew potatoes who treat worship as a box to check, while leaving leaders discouraged by shallow commitment. In addition, the growing professional credentialing requirements for pastors have led to fewer laity feeling empowered or equipped to lead ministries. (For more information on "reclaiming the call of lay ministry," see Kotan's and Bradford's book, *IMPACT! Reclaiming the Call of Lay Ministry.)*[117]

[117] Kay Kotan and Blake Bradford, *Impact! Reclaiming the Call of Lay Ministry* (Market Square Books, 2018).

Leader*ship* for Disciple*ship* at the Port of Call

As a church shifts its disciple*ship* "course" to a more holistic, relation*ship*-based approach, some shifts will be needed in the training and equipping ministry leader*ship*. Gone are the days when only scholars taught "disciple*ship*." This approach is not sustainable, scalable, or biblical. If this were the case, Jesus would not have deployed his disciples two by two. He would have assumed responsibility for all the teaching and healing while they observed. Jesus knew he would not be here on earth forever, so he modeled a plan of relational disciple*ship* that common (lay) people learned and then led.

In a relation*ship*-centered disciple*ship* approach, ministry leaders are not the doers of ministry. To make the needed shifts, churches will need to resist the myth that hiring staff is the go-to solution for growing a ministry area. Again, this approach is not sustainable nor biblical and is destined for failure sooner or later. Instead, ensure your ministry team leader*ship* is first and foremost team builders. A team-building mindset is the number one proven gift needed for a ministry team leader in a healthy, vital relational disciple*ship* approach. A culture of staff and unpaid leaders building teams rather than doing ministry themselves is key to a church's disciple*ship* growth and multiplication. It is the distinction between offering a navigation system and a compass. A navigation system provides detailed steps and a predetermined course for the journey. However, a compass merely provides direction, allowing people to choose their specific pathway and decisions along the journey towards the lighthouse and the disciple*ship* pathway.

Ministry Leader*ship*'s primary role is to:

- Identify disciples to serve.
- Recruit disciples who are gifted and passionate for the ministry area.

- Equip the ministry team's disciples for the ministry.
- Deploy the disciples to serve.
- Coordinate missionally aligned and effective ministry.

Leader*ship* Development at the Port of Call

Leader*ship* is one of the three keys to becoming a preferred port of call, along with relation*ships* and disciple*ship*. One particularly important part of leader*ship* is the ongoing development of both new and existing leaders. This development must be intentional in its process and its investment. Specific leader*ship* development pathways must be in place to identify potential new and existing leaders for elected administrative committees and for ministry leader*ship* (pastors, paid staff, and unpaid ministry team leaders). There must also be a financial investment in leader*ship*. This includes team development activities, team and individual retreats, leader*ship* resources, conferences, webinars, and so on.

Ships cannot guide themselves into or out of ports of call or have the ability to resource all their own needs while in port. Even the largest, self-sustaining vessels need a tugboat to help them maneuver safely, harbor stewards to assist with logistics, and the port authority to provide order and communication for those navigating the harbor.

Pastors and leaders, like tugboats, harbor stewards, and port authority officials, need continuous development to navigate new challenges, currents, and crowded harbors. Leader*ship* development ensures that tugboats, harbor stewards, and port authority officials (pastors, ministry leaders, and members of the leader*ship* board) are:

- Strong enough for the task (skills, spiritual maturity).
- Knowledgeable about hidden dangers (wisdom, discernment).

- Equipped to serve both the harbor (church) and the open waters (mission field).
- Able and willing to learn to read the waters: discern cultural tides, generational shifts, and congregational needs.
- Modeling servant leader*ship* by pulling, not pushing.
- Providing safe waters for training, reflection, and sharpening.
- Acting as a hub where new tugboats, harbor stewards, and port authorities (emerging leaders) are equipped.
- Aligning its structures and systems to nurture growth rather than obstruct it.
- Providing real-world practice for leader*ship*.
- Engaging with different "ships," leader*ship* develops flexibility and empathy.

Leader*ship* development is the continual strengthening of tugboats, harbor stewards, and port authorities to attain the port of call's mission. Leader*ship* development ensures there are enough qualified and committed tugboats, harbor stewards, and port authorities to guide more ships safely in and out of harbors, multiplying the reach of the Kingdom across the seas. A harbor full of docked ships has no Kingdom impact until vessels return to open waters. Missional fulfillment requires movement.

When a port of call (church) invests in ongoing leader*ship* development:

- Ships (people) are mobilized into their God-given callings.
- Harbors (churches) remain places of renewal, not bottlenecks.
- The wider seas (the world) are filled with more vessels carrying Kingdom cargo.

If your church is looking for a launching point to develop a leader*ship* development process, check out Kotan's book, *Launching Leaders: Taking Leadership Development to New Heights,* and the associated webinar.[118]

Leader*ship* and Missional Accountability at the Port of Call

Effective leader*ship* boards, pastors, and ministry team leaders know the value of accountability and practice it. Rather than seeing accountability as a four-letter word, effective leader*ship* engages in the accountable leader*ship* model. Accountable leader*ship* combines responsibility and authority for missional effectiveness, alignment, and impact. This valuable leader*ship* tool is utilized to focus, evaluate, empower, encourage, coach, and direct team members and the overall ministry. The Accountable Leader*ship* Cycle below was created by authors Kay Kotan and Blake Bradford as a tool for leader*ship* to practice accountable leader*ship*. (For a deeper dive into accountable leader*ship* and the Accountable Leader*ship* Cycle, see Mission Possible 3.)[119]

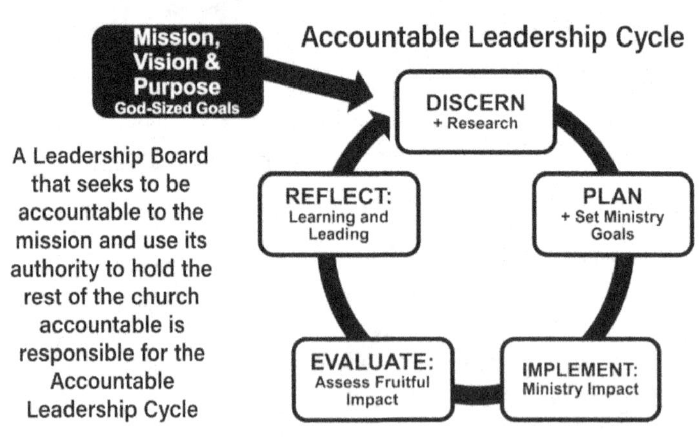

[118] Kay Kotan and Phil Schroeder, *Launching Leaders: Taking Leadership Development to New Heights* (Market Square Books, 2019) and "Launching Leaders Webinar," video webinar, https://kaykotan.com.

[119] Kay Kotan and Blake Bradford, *Mission Possible 3: Expanded 3rd Edition* (Market Square Books, 2019).

Key Points

1. The changing winds of culture require a different model of leader*ship* for missional fruitfulness and effectiveness.

2. To implement relation*ship*-based disciple*ship,* the understanding and approach of leader*ship* will need to shift dramatically away from traditional models.

3. Church leaders must be continuously adapting, learning, relearning, and unlearning. They require flexibility, humbleness, adaptability, and accountability as servant leaders.

4. The port authority (the church's leader*ship* board) is responsible for aligning resources and mission.

5. A pastor (escort tugboat) guides people (ships) into the harbor (church) for rest, renewal, and alignment, and then escorts them back out to sea (the mission field) for Kingdom impact.

6. Ministry team leaders (harbor stewards) are to identify, equip, recruit, and deploy people (ships).

7. Gone are the days of scholars being the only ones responsible for disciple*ship* development and teaching.

8. Ongoing leader*ship* development is a required practice of intentionality and investment.

9. Effective leader*ship* boards, pastors, and ministry teams know the value of accountability and practice it.

Case Study

The church facilities were those that most church leaders only dream about. They included a modern, accessible church building, a newer secondary building with a gym, a commercial kitchen, ample classroom space, and parking to accommodate endless growth. The surrounding community was chock-full of need, potential, and possibility. The pastor and a handful of leaders recognized the gaps between the church and the community and were willing to pursue missional alignment.

The congregation, unfortunately, was half the size it was just a few years ago. Stuck in a mindset of fear and scarcity, the congregation was floundering. They were unwilling to let go of ineffective ministries for the sake of historical preservation. Their fear of losing more people stifled any innovation. Their scarcity mindset paralyzed them from making even the slightest needed changes. Steeped in the value and practice of keeping the remaining congregation happy and comfortable, the church continued its decline in engagement and financial resources. Even the leaders who desired a new pathway forward grew less willing to vocalize their thoughts, offer help, or persist in resisting the scarcity and seemingly entrenched congregation. These leaders found the resistance impenetrable. The pastor requested a new appointment.

Many leaders today are abandoning their leader*ship* posts, and some are even leaving the church. Those that remain are happy (for the time being) and comfortable (no changes have been made). The community's needs have gone unmet. Those looking for hope, love, and community are still searching.

While we could offer stories with different, happier outcomes, we offer this story for reflection and consideration. Thousands of churches in America close every year. Thousands of church buildings are sold and repurposed. The country is becoming increasingly unchurched, while the church is becoming increasingly irrelevant and untrustworthy. If our towns and cities are going to become more like heaven on earth, it will take a change in the culture of church leader*ship.* Church leaders will need to be willing to navigate rather than skirt conflict. They will need to become resilient leaders and make tough decisions, even if it means some pruning today for future growth and fruit. We hope the story of this church, like so many across the country, might inspire leader*ship* to risk more for the sake of the Kingdom.

CHAPTER EIGHT

New Orbital Port Vitality Measurements

Whenever, though, they turn to face God as Moses did, God removes the veil and there they are—face-to-face! They suddenly recognize that God is a living, personal presence, not a piece of chiseled stone. And when God is personally present, a living Spirit, that old, constricting legislation is recognized as obsolete. We're free of it! All of us! Nothing between us and God, our faces shining with the brightness of his face. And so we are transfigured much like the Messiah, our lives gradually becoming brighter and more beautiful as God enters our lives and we become like him.

2 Corinthians 3:17 (MSG)

Reflect on the scripture above for a moment. Disciples experience the fullness of Christ and are profoundly transformed by the presence of the Holy Spirit as God enters a disciple's life. How is this type of transformation recognized and measured in a church's disciple*ship* pathway? How would more disciples in the church who are transformed in this way lead to a more relational community or have a greater impact in and with the community for the Kingdom's sake?

Why Some Vitality Metrics Are Outdated and Irrelevant

For decades (if not centuries), there has been a great debate over how to measure the health and vitality of churches and their congregants. Should such measurements be qualitative or quantitative? Perhaps both? What measurements reveal the most mission-critical information to analyze and indicate health? How do we know if people are growing in their relationships with Christ? How do we know if the church is growing in the number of new people reached and in its Kingdom impact in the greater community?

There are two types of measurements or indicators: lag and lead. Lag measures reflect past performance and outcomes, while lead measures are predictive and focus on actions that influence future results. Lag measures tell you what happened, while lead measures tell you what actions will likely lead to desired outcomes. Historically, the majority of the measurements churches have used up until now have been lag measurements. Because churches are familiar with analyzing lag indicators, they struggle to understand and implement lead indicators and strategies. Churches have primarily relied on measuring results (membership) rather than on effective methods for building new relation*ships*, new disciples, growth in disciple*ship*, and new leaders and leader*ship* development.

Why Do We Need a New Scorecard?

Do we value what we measure, or do we measure what we value? This is not a play on words. What is simple to measure and what we're asked to measure often ends up being what we value most. We frequently equate value with measurability—especially when it's something we're required to measure. Take the time to ask these two questions: What is of true value, and for whom is it valuable? Then, measure that.

In his book *Missional Renaissance: Changing the Scorecard for the Church*, Reggie McNeal states, "In a program-driven church, we track participation. In a people development culture, the key issue is maturation. Are people growing in every aspect of their lives? Are they becoming more like Jesus? Are they blessing the world as the people of God?"[120]

But again, in light of this, for whom are these stats important? If the stats are important for the local ministry, this is a benchmark. However, oftentimes, an unintended consequence of having to share monthly statistics with those in judicatory leader*ship* is to 1: tempt church leaders to be disingenuous, or 2: view each meaningful encounter as a check mark on the report card rather than relation*ship*-building. Regardless of what denominational bodies ask them to track, local church leaders need to prayerfully determine the measures of vitality that are most relevant to their context. If there is no commitment, understanding, or buy-in that the markers are meaningful and affect how we plan, spend, and focus, it won't matter what we measure!

Why Do We Even Need Stats?

One privilege The Salvation Army enjoys is a partnership with others who provide funds to help fulfill its mission. By doing so, the partners join in that mission. Unlike other churches, The Salvation Army does not survive financially on the tithes and offerings of those who call it their church. However, they do rely on those financial partners such as donors, grantors, and public funds. Funders require statistics to show how their money has been used, and this information is equally important for The Salvation Army's leader*ship* to exercise responsible stewardship.

Churches in other denominations (not The Salvation Army) and nondenominational churches used to rely solely on offerings. However, an increasing number of churches are struggling with financial sustainability using this single-source, offering-plate strategy. What could others learn and apply from The Salvation

[120] Reggie McNeal, *Missional Renaissance: Changing the Scorecard for the Church* (Jossey-Bass, February 3, 2009).

Army model—especially its thrift store model, which helps fund its social ministries and adult rehabilitation centers?

While membership, worship attendance, and finances have been the primary indicators of vitality, we question whether they should ever have been the measure of fruitfulness, effectiveness, and vitality. Since church leaders tend to focus on what we (or our denomination/judicatory leaders) measure, has measuring these three things contributed to our decline and lack of vitality?

Many of the current statistics churches are asked to track communicate a very loud message from judicatory leader*ship*: "We don't trust you and question everything you're doing." There are increasing questions about why certain statistics are necessary. For whom are they important? For example, The Salvation Army's judicatory leaders have entrusted a flock of souls, a community to represent, a building to maintain, and a budget to manage. Yet it is the local leader*ship* who benefit most from the gathered stats. As such, it is a "fruit inspection" tool for monitoring progress. The tool can indicate whether something needs to be improved or changed. It can also serve as proof of success and justification for a grantor to partner with the local corps or church in ministry.

Does Measurement Even Matter?

Because knowing what and how to measure has become confusing and vague, many churches simply no longer measure anything. As long as there are enough dollars to keep the lights on and keep the existing people happy, they are good to go.

Organizations may not consistently measure effectiveness due to various factors, including resistance to measurement, flawed or overly simplistic metrics, unclear goals, and challenges in data collection and analysis. Another prominent reason for inconsistent measurement is a lack of understanding of how the information is used, why it is important to collect, and how the data can be useful at the local level. These issues can lead to ineffective evaluations, wasted resources, and potentially hinder organizational improvement.

Churches are organizations that exist for the primary benefit of nonmembers. Many people hold the view that churches exist primarily to serve the needs of their communities and to spread their spiritual message rather than for self-serving financial gain. Yet most of the measurements churches use are focused on members (those who are part of the congregation, whether technically members or not). Churches struggle to identify lag (let alone lead) measures when it comes to their impact in the community. There is a mammoth disconnect.

What Is Critically Important to Measure?

Let's first look at another nonprofit entity as an example, a local school board. Picture a meeting where elected school board members ask the superintendent for statistics on whether or not children are learning. Imagine what might happen if the superintendent had no clue whether the students in the district were learning and progressing as needed. That superintendent instead shares that students are happy and having a good time. How long do you think the superintendent would keep his job? A school's primary purpose is to teach students. If the highest-ranking leader can't answer this simple question, there is a huge problem. The same is true for private enterprises. If the president or chief executive officer is unable to report on any financial indicators of health and profitability to the board and its shareholders, that person would be fired. Without measuring whether an organization's vitality aligns with its purpose, leading effectively and making strategic decisions becomes difficult—if not impossible.

Because Jesus defined every church's mission—to make disciples who transform their community and world—measuring missional effectiveness is essential. While many churches find this challenging, as we noted earlier, the difficulty does not mean churches get a pass.

If a ship were to measure only it's schedule adherence, voyage duration, fuel consumption and speed, these metrics would be meaningless if it did not include cargo delivery, quantity accuracy and condition compliance. Similarly, an organization can't stay afloat and accomplish its mission without continuously analyzing its effectiveness and making the necessary adjustments. As an overarching measurement strategy, the following need to be measured in some way:

- The church's missional effectiveness through growing relation*ships*
- People's growth in their disciple*ship* journey (knowing, loving, following, and behaving more and more like Jesus)
- People's overall well-being, inside and outside the church
- The church's development in raising up leaders and the people's development in leader*ship*
- A growing positive impact on the greater community (knowing, serving, connecting) that results in a better community

Measuring Church Health

Let's start with the measurement of church health and vitality. Knowing whether the church is missionally effective is important, but how we measure it often leads to controversy. For starters, the common measurements have shifted over time. While the growth or decline in membership used to be the go-to metric, most agree it is no longer the most effective measurement. Growing a membership roster does not indicate that people are growing in their disciple*ship* or if the church is making an impact on the community. It only takes a glance at the percentage of the membership rolls in the majority of churches that have been in existence for more than twenty to twenty-five years to know membership is usually not a very helpful measurement. These churches likely have only 20 to 50 percent of those on their membership rolls actively engaged in the church at any level.

The other popular vitality metric is a church's average worship attendance. Yet, there is an ongoing debate about using average worship attendance as a vitality metric because it does not necessarily reflect individuals' disciple*ship* growth, community impact, or relational growth. While some still use this metric, it is becoming less of a focus for most. One reason for shifting away from measuring worship attendance is the declining frequency of worship attendance over the past few decades. Another reason churches no longer use this as a vitality marker is due to the inconsistencies and discrepancies in counting from church to church and from leader to leader. To further complicate counting worship attendance, there are various, conflicting definitions for measuring the increasing number of online ministries. For example, some churches count a view of ten or more minutes as "attendance," while others count any amount of viewing time (e.g., a few seconds). Yet others use a 1.5 to 2.5 multiplier for every view to factor in the potential for multiple people viewing on one device.

Whether it is measuring membership or average worship attendance, there is another common pushback against using either of these metrics. Many churches are seeing increases in these two common metrics due to membership transfers. Church membership transfers occur for a variety of reasons. Some people move from one location to another because of job changes or retirement. Others move their membership from one church to another (often within the same denomination) due to urban or suburban sprawl, a new pastoral appointment, a congregational conflict, or changing neighborhood demographics. If a church is growing primarily through membership transfers, it is not reaching new people. "Growth" by membership transfers is often a false vitality marker. The proverbial sheep are simply changing their pen of choice (preferred port of call). Transfer growth does not address the growing number of Nones and the multiple generations of families who have never been a part of a faith community.

Measuring Relation*ship* Growth

We hope by now that it is abundantly clear that we believe relation*ships* are the gateway to a healthy, vital church. This includes consistently building new relation*ships* within the greater community, disciples developing a deeper relation*ship* with Christ, and building healthy relation*ships* amongst disciples. The keys for measuring these types of relation*ships* include both the quantity of relation*ships* the church (preferred port of call) builds and its disciples (becoming a disciple-maker), as well as the deepening of those relation*ships* (disciple*ship,* evangelism, and leader*ship).*

While it may take more resources to develop a system for measuring relation*ship* growth, it will be well worth the effort. When deepening existing and building new relation*ships* becomes a focus, more attention, resources, and effort will be invested in relation*ships.*

Take a look back in Chapter 6 at the orbital model. In this model, the vitality markers are measured by the number of people in orbit and the relational movements among them. For example, more churched disciples are serving in the neighborhood school's reading program (building relation*ships* with new people). By serving, the disciples are growing in their relation*ship* with Christ. Through that relation*ship*-building, a student from the school's reading program and her family attend the church's trunk-or-treat community event.

To measure relation*ship* growth and vitality, the church must have some means to track a growing influence, the number of new relation*ships*, and their ongoing growth.

Measuring Disciple*ship* Growth

Now let's take a look at measurements related to individuals' disciple*ship* journeys. How does a church measure the spiritual growth of its congregants? Some would suggest tracking the number of people participating in a small group or Sunday school. Or those serving in some sort of hands-on mission. Or measuring the generosity (tithes and offerings). Yet, once again, how these are counted varies from church to church, pastor to pastor, or even from one volunteer to another in the same church. The inconsistencies are endless. In addition, if the total number is all that is being tracked, how would church leaders know if there is only a revolving door of different people? How would leaders know if people are staying and growing in the various ministry opportunities? Is a person growing in their disciple*ship* if they don't stay consistently engaged?

Another issue in measuring disciple*ship* growth is the lack of having, implementing, communicating, and aligning people and ministry opportunities with a disciple*ship* pathway. If the church's purpose is to help people grow in their relation*ship* with Christ, but there is no identifiable pathway, how would a person or the church know if they are growing? What are the disciple*ship* growth indicators? How are the ministries intentionally and clearly aligned with the disciple*ship* pathway? How do people engage in their disciple*ship* journeys?

I (Kay) once served on a judicatory committee tasked with developing congregational training to help church leaders create and implement disciple*ship* pathways. The committee struggled with its assignment. Over six months were spent arguing over the definition of a disciple before we could even begin to work on a disciple*ship* pathway. I believe we make it much harder, more confusing, and more complex than it needs to be!

As someone who has invested considerable time in my church consulting and coaching on the topic of simplified, accountable structure,[121] I (Kay) would be remiss if I didn't identify the connection between measuring church vitality and health and a church's structure and accountable leader*ship*. I often ask the leader*ship* boards and councils I work with this question: How frequently do you ask about the church's missional effectiveness? While church leaders spend hours every month in meetings, most administrative committees and ministry teams don't ask themselves this vital question. Unfortunately, even if this question emerges, leaders wrestle with how to discern and measure the missional effectiveness of their church and ministries. Imagine the outcome if any other existing organization had no clear indication of whether or not it was fulfilling its purpose. They would likely not exist. Yet, this is not uncommon for churches. Maybe this is one of the major reasons for the church's decline ...

Measuring Leader*ship* Growth

While the church once developed leaders to serve in the secular world, the church now depends on secular leaders to become part of the church and serve in leader*ship*. As mentioned in Chapter 7, an intentional leader*ship* development pathway needs to be in place before leader*shi*p development can occur. Once the pathway for leader*ship* development is in place,

---

[121] Kotan and Bradford, *Mission Possible 3* and *Kay Kotan, SAS-2: Systems Assessment Snapshot*, https://kaykotan.com/sas-2.

there are a few key factors to measure the health and vitality of your leader*ship*. A healthy, vital church has a healthy leader*ship* culture when:

- There is a continuous leader*ship* development process in place.
- There is a continuous stream of new disciples entering the leader*ship* development process.
- There is a growing number of leaders to serve in the church, the community, and in the marketplace.
- There is a growing number of maturing disciples who are also servant leaders.
- Accountability leader*ship* is expected, respected, and identified as a key trait of healthy, vital leader*ship* in healthy, vital churches.

To measure the health and vitality of leader*ship* means to track the number of leaders entering leader*ship* development, the number serving as leaders (in all capacities), the number investing in new leaders, and the deepening skills, wisdom, and influence of the leaders.

Some Measurement Concepts to Consider

There is no one best method or one "right" measurement for all churches. The most critical consideration when discerning the best way to measure vitality and growth is to include both lead and lag indicators and measure the growth and impact in relation*ships*, disciple*ship*, and leader*ship*. In summary, ensure the number of people associated with the church is growing (relation*ships*), and those associated people are continuously growing in their disciple*ship* and leader*ship*. When there is growth and development in relation*ships*, disciple*ship*, and leader*ship*, there is movement. One might even suggest that a movement is the result of church health and vitality.

As we mentioned in Chapter 6, we must move away from a programmatic, Sunday-centric approach to measure vitality and health. Instead of starting with program development, healthy and vital churches understand that the number of people the church influences and the number who are growing deeper in their relation*ship* with Jesus Christ are key. Healthy, vital churches concentrate more on building new relation*ships* and helping people grow in their relation*ship* with Christ (disciple*ship* and leader*ship),* resulting in the transformation of people and their communities.

Below are other options for assessing and measuring health and vitality. Take a look at each to understand the overall concepts of healthy measurements. You might find one model that fits your church like a glove. Or, you may find that tweaking a model is a solution for your church. Or, you might combine concepts from two or three models to create a unique assessment for vitality and effectiveness.

No matter which model you choose or create, let's first agree on a key concept for growth and vitality. This key concept is understanding that healthy things grow and multiply. This means that new relation*ships* are constantly being built, and people are moving through a process (a movement) to become more and more like Jesus (disciple*ship* and leader*ship)* and inviting new people on the journey (disciple*ship).* Stagnant organizations experience a range of negative consequences, including decreased innovation, lower engagement, missed opportunities, and ultimately, a decline in vitality and missional effectiveness. These issues stem from a lack of adaptation to change, outdated processes, and a failure to nurture growth and development in relation*ships,* disciple*ship,* and leader*ship.*

The Dimensions of Thriving Churches & Flourishing People

So, what do disconnected, lonely, isolated individuals truly need to find belonging, purpose, and a sense of impact—to truly thrive (as introduced in Chapters 1 and 2)? A church might decide its vitality markers are based on personal growth, emotional well-being, relation*ships*, purpose, and overall health, or it might incorporate these factors into other models.

These dimensions are important for achieving balance and happiness in life.

In their State of the Church research,[122] Barna asked two key questions—the first question about church health, and the second about the overall well-being of its people.

1. Thriving churches: How healthy and effective is our church?
2. Flourishing people: How are our people doing in terms of overall well-being?

Barna saw trends in how these two key measurements are interrelated. Thriving churches raise up flourishing people, and flourishing people make up thriving churches.

Barna's fifteen dimensions of thriving churches are identified and defined below. Notice that there are three categories identified within these fifteen dimensions of thriving churches, and notice how they mirror the development of relation*ships,* disciple*ship,* and leader*ship* that we have focused on in this resource.

---

[122] Barna Group, "Barna Researchers Introduce Dimensions of Flourishing" (video), accessed November 19, 2025, https://barna.gloo.us/videos/barna-researchers-introduce-dimensions-of-flourishing.

The Fifteen Dimensions of Thriving Churches

Nurturing the Congregation

1. **Connected Community:** Fostering a sense of belonging and meaningful relation*ships* among members.
2. **Prayer Culture:** Encouraging and facilitating consistent prayer within the church community.
3. **Spiritual Formation:** Providing opportunities for individuals to grow in their faith and relation*ship* with God.
4. **Worship Experience:** Creating meaningful and transformative worship services.
5. **Bible Centeredness:** Emphasizing the importance of the Bible in teaching and daily life.
6. **Trusted Leaders:** Developing leaders who are respected, trustworthy, and effective.

Sending People Out

7. **Faith Sharing:** Equipping and encouraging members to share their faith with others.
8. **Holistic Stewardship:** Promoting responsible management of resources and finances.
9. **Social Impact:** Engaging in activities that benefit the wider community.
10. **Serving Others:** Providing opportunities for members to serve within and outside the church.

Strengthening Leader*ship* and Operations

11. **Leader*ship* Development:** Investing in the growth and development of current and future leaders.

12. **Future Focused:** Planning and preparing for the future, including adapting to changing needs and trends.

13. **Resource Stability:** Ensuring the church has the necessary resources to fulfill its mission.

14. **Data Informed:** Utilizing data to make informed decisions and track progress.

15. **Team Health:** Fostering a healthy and effective team environment within the church.

The following are the dimensions identified by Barna as characteristic of flourishing people.

The Five Dimensions of Flourishing People

1. Faith

2. Finances

3. Relation*ships*

4. Physical and mental health

5. Vocation

Through their research and analysis, Barna identified this connection to churches and their people: "People who are engaged with a church community and have a healthy faith are more likely to be flourishing personally across all dimensions of human flourishing."[123] These dimensions, when addressed effectively, contribute to a church that is both spiritually healthy and impactful in its community.

Here is a deeper dive into the five dimensions of flourishing people. As you read, notice how the dimensions line up with so many of the mental health concerns and the needs and desires of moms, the Nones, and Gen Z identified in Chapter 1. Consider how understanding and helping people develop in each dimension can serve as a bridge for relation*ships,* disciple*ship,* and leader*ship* inside and outside your church.

Faith

Disciples can build relation*ships* with seekers by living out their faith authentically and transparently. Rather than leading with doctrine, they can share how their spiritual beliefs shape their everyday decisions, give them peace, and inspire purposeful living. Personal stories of transformation, answered prayers, or spiritual growth often speak louder than abstract teachings. Instead of pressuring seekers, disciples can create safe, invitational spaces for curiosity and exploration—inviting seekers into prayer, worship, or spiritual conversations when appropriate. This approach helps seekers see faith not as a rigid system but as a living, relational journey they might want to explore.

Finances

Disciples can model wise financial stewardship, contentment, and generosity in ways that reflect a deeper trust in God. Rather than focusing on wealth or success, they can demonstrate how financial peace and freedom come from managing resources well and living with open hands. When appropriate, followers of Christ can provide tangible support to

---

[123] Barna Group, "Barna Researchers Introduce Dimensions of Flourishing."

seekers in need—whether through giving, budgeting help, or sharing resources—without condescension or obligation. This practical kindness reflects the heart of the gospel and builds credibility and trust in relation*ships*.

Relation*ships*

Building meaningful connections is foundational to disciple*ship*. Disciples can invest in relation*ships* with seekers by showing up consistently, listening well, and being genuinely present. Practicing hospitality—inviting someone to coffee, sharing meals, or celebrating important life events—goes a long way toward building trust. Disciples can also offer emotional support and a nonjudgmental presence, making it clear that seekers are loved and valued as they are. A posture of curiosity and respect will open doors to greater trust and vulnerability. Through steady and sincere relation*ships*, disciples earn the right to speak into the deeper parts of a seeker's life.

Physical and Mental Health

Holistic well-being is a part of a faithful life. By being open about their own challenges and growth in areas like stress, anxiety, rest, and fitness, believers create space for honest dialogue. They can also recognize when a seeker is struggling and respond with empathy rather than spiritual clichés. Offering to pray, walk together, or connect them to helpful resources shows that faith speaks to real-life issues. This dimension reminds seekers that God cares not only for their souls but for their bodies and minds as well.

Vocation

In the area of work and calling, Christ-followers can support seekers by affirming their gifts and helping them discover how their talents and passions connect to a greater purpose. Many people wrestle with identity and meaning in their careers, and disciples can offer encouragement by highlighting how all work has dignity and can be an expression of service and impact. When seekers face job loss, burnout, or vocational uncertainty, believers can come alongside them with wisdom, prayer, and practical guidance—showing that God cares deeply about what they do and who they are becoming through it.

Addressing the disconnect of churches and the postmodern culture present today cannot happen just through quoting Bible verses; it happens by living out our faith across every aspect of life, offering real companionship, hope, and love in ways that resonate deeply with the human experience.

This research can be yet another tool or model of measuring effectiveness and vitality. It could be a standalone metric, or it could be incorporated into one of the other models. For example, a church could use the orbital model and overlay the thriving and flourishing markers onto the relation*ship,* disciple*ship,* and leader*ship* development pathways. Barna offers resources and assessments on this model in their Church Pulse resources.[124]

The Frequency of Reporting

The benefit of reporting vitality markers monthly allows for a more accurate memory of what has recently occurred. The challenge is that keeping stats can take an inordinate amount of time each month, both locally and at the judicatory level.

As a best practice for the local church, the governing board will monitor the dashboard for church vitality and growing disciples each month. If markers are not being met, there is an accountability conversation with the pastor to help identify

---

[124] Barna Group, "A Quick Guide to the ChurchPulse Assessment," accessed November 19, 2025, https://f.hubspotusercontent10.net/hubfs/2568162/Knowledge%20Center%20Resources/Church%20Pulse%20Quick%20Guide.pdf.

obstacles or issues that need to be resolved for vitality and health to prevail.

Whatever statistics are measured, who measures them, and how often they are reported do matter. But what matters most is that the church and its leaders track what shifts the church forward most effectively, leverage the church's resources most efficiently, and provide indicators if the church is being missionally effective. The endgame is not the reporting. The endgame is to monitor the church's activities through data collection to ensure it is living out its purpose as mandated by the Great Commission and the Great Commandment.

Wrap-Up

It has been proven again and again that what an organization measures becomes its focus. This means that we must be measuring the right things. Otherwise, the church risks investing in activities that do not bear fruit or contribute to the health and vitality of the church itself, the growth of its disciples, or the well-being of the community it is called to serve. What you measure matters! Be intentional and diligent in choosing what your church measures. Be intentional about the mission—and vision-based reasons for the measurements. Measure accurately. Use the data collected to make the necessary shifts to achieve the intended, missional outcomes of the measurements.

Key Points

1. Not all data points and measurements are helpful, relevant, or needed in the church of today. Don't measure simply for the sake of a measuring task. Measure activities and outcomes that drive your church's mission and vision.

2. These four aspects of ministry need to be measured:

   a. The church's missional effectiveness through growing relation*ships*

   b. People's growth in their disciple*ship* journey (knowing, loving, following, and behaving more and more like Jesus)

   c. People's overall well-being, inside and outside the church

   d. The church's development in raising up leaders and the people's development in leader*ship*

   e. A growing positive impact on the greater community (knowing, serving, connecting) that results in a better community

3. Focused and intentional church systems need to be in place to facilitate the desired missional outcomes, such as a disciple*ship* pathway, a leader*ship* development process, and intentional methods for building relation*ships*.

4. Focused and intentional ministries need to be in place to drive the desired missional outcomes, such as an evangelism team, a leader*ship* development team (the nominations committee in the United Methodist Church and Pastoral Care Council in The Salvation Army), and a disciple*ship* team that points disciples to the disciple*ship* pathway and coordinates ministries and growth opportunities to support and grow disciples.

5. Being the church means your top priority is new and growing relation*ships*.

   a. Continuously building new relation*ships* with neighbors in the mission field

b. Continuously helping people grow in their relationship with Jesus and become more Christlike (disciple*ship).*

c. Continuously building the skills, confidence, and commitment of leaders to serve, grow the church, and reach new people for Christ (leader*ship).*

d. Continuously creating new relation*ships* and building existing relation*ships* with community leaders and influencers to maintain a deep understanding of the people who make up the community you're called to reach.

Case Study

A Look at a Sample Scorecard

As a divisional commander in The Salvation Army, I (Major Kelly Collins) created a "new scorecard" for her corps officers (local pastors). The following is a rundown of the types of data to collect, why this data is important, and the shift in how health and vitality are measured using this new scorecard.

If gathering statistics is primarily important to local leader*ship*, more members of the leader*ship* team need easy access to input data. Ideally, an app could be created that corps officers could grant (and block, if/when necessary) access to soldiers (congregants), volunteers, and employees. Those at divisional headquarters (similar to conferences in the United Methodist Church) and territorial headquarters (similar to jurisdictions in the United Methodist Church) who need this information could also have access—streamlining the process. There are multiple apps already in existence that are similar.

What Needs to be Tracked?

	Sun	M	T	W	Th	F	Sat
Meaningful Ministry Connections							
Those initiating the connections							
Those receiving the connections							
Definition/Purpose: Making relation*ships* deeper. Two-way conversations that 1. Gain new information 2. Move people closer to Jesus 3. Help people get more missionally involved with the community Examples: Meaningful conversations (face to face, text, video, etc.) & praying with and for people · Worship (definition: Gathering to encounter God. Focus is on God through testimonies, praise, and proclamation) · Engaging with others outside of the four walls of the corps (church) building							
	Sun	M	T	W	Th	F	Sat
Persons Served							
Those serving							
Those being served							
Definition/Purpose: Public and private ministry touchpoints. Examples, but not limited to: · Social Ministries, Emergency Assistance · Service "projects"							

	Sun	M	T	W	Th	F	Sat
Discipleship							
Those discipling							
Those being discipled							
Definition/Purpose: Ongoing growth in faith. Implies commitment. Examples, but not limited to: Bible study disciple*ship* group, small group, Sunday school, character building, mentoring, devotions, Vacation Bible Schoo							
	Sun	M	T	W	Th	F	Sat
Community Partnerships							
SA Partner							
Community Partner (counted as a group)							
Definition/Purpose: Collaboration with other community groups with a goal of enhancing our Mission. Examples, but not limited to: other churches, local schools, chamber of commerce, Economic Development Corp, other local social services organizations, local business leaders, local community leaders (police, fire, mayor, city council, libraries, medical personnel).							

Each section of the example above encompasses all five facets of The Salvation Army's mission. If activities and ministries don't align with the mission, leaders should not engage in them. This helps clearly align priorities and focus.

This measure intentionally does not include membership, rentals of church facilities without meaningful ministry connections (missional focus), or specific leader*ship* development, since empowering the church to do these things is in itself leader*shi*p development.

CHAPTER NINE

Charting the Course for Establishing a Healthy Harbor

You have now been introduced to a new model for shaping the life of your church and why this reshaping is important. Now that you have a deeper understanding of the orbital port model and why a shift in course is needed, let's integrate the tools and insights provided in this resource and see how they can be incorporated into your healthy, vital preferred port of call (church).

The Crisis of Relation*ships*

Provided in the first chapter of this book was a shipload of information detailing the various crises in people's relation*ships*. We also outlined how a lack of authentic relation*ships* and community has affected critical aspects of life, such as the mental health crisis, the growing populations of Nones, moms experiencing isolation and stress, and the hurt and distrust Gen Z has experienced with the church.

No port of call (church) can address all of these relational concerns. However, the church must step up and be a part of this national emergency. Which relation*ship* crisis would your port of call (church) be willing to address, inviting other relation*ships* into your harbor and orbit to relieve just one percent of this country's relational crisis?

The Disconnected Orbits

Chapter 2 reminded the church of how it has become disconnected from its harbor (mission field) and its relation*ships* (people). In addition, this chapter described the disconnection between the church's orbits and the orbits of relation*ships* (people) who are desperately trying to navigate the rough seas of life.

This chapter challenges the church to examine its port's orbits as well as the individual relation*ships* orbits of the people who currently refer to the church as their preferred port of call. What might need to be remodeled, reimagined, stopped, or started in these orbits so that the church becomes the preferred port of call for those ships currently lost at sea? How might your port of call need to reconsider current values, spending habits, historical programs, and unintentional barriers for new relation*ship* possibilities?

Building New Relation*ships* (Community)

Every church desires to be the central hub of the community—the preferred port of call in your harbor. In Chapter 3, we identified why building new relation*ships*—intentionally locating and then lovingly, gracefully intersecting with other ships' orbits (their currently preferred activities and rhythms of life). Eventually, through the building of relation*ships* and the intersecting orbits, we may have the honor to invite those relation*ships* into the port of call (church's) orbits of relation*ship,* disciple*ship,* and leader*ship.* This chapter challenges the church, its disciples, and its leaders to rethink their overall approach to becoming a preferred port of call. This includes revisiting the why and the how, as well as finances, innovation, cultural competence, and emotional competence. What new awarenesses were realized from this chapter, and how might they be addressed to become a preferred port of call with Kingdom impact?

Relational Disciple*ship*

The understanding of and approach to disciple*ship* were challenged in Chapter 4. The focus was on gaining a comprehensive description of discipling, developing a disciple*ship* pathway, intentionally focusing on disciple*ship* development, and understanding how relation*ships* and disciple*ship* intersect. This chapter calls the church's attention to the centrality of disciple*ship* in the life of the port of call (the church). Given the spiritual openness of the unchurched, having a clear path of disciple*ship* through relation*ships* is essential. How does your church intentionally disciple people? How central is disciple*ship* development in the life of your church?

New Relation*ship* Orbits

In Chapter 5, we focused on how growing churches build new spiritual communities and why declining churches struggle to do so, including by building new relation*ships*. Several innovative models for building new spiritual communities were offered for your consideration and to spark new port innovation. What connected with you in this chapter? How did the Holy Spirit ignite your imagination? How is God calling you into a new future as the preferred port of call to reach more ships?

Disciple*ship* for the Orbital Port

A disciple*ship* pathway, as we saw in Chapter 6, is essential for guiding people in their spiritual journey and aligning the church around its mission. Rather than striving for a "perfect" plan, it is more important to establish a clear, intentional pathway that directs disciple*ship*, relation*ships*, and leader*ship* development. When these pathways overlap and are supported by vitality markers, they provide clarity for decision-making and resource allocation. To achieve the desired missional outcomes, churches must develop intentional systems—such as disciple*ship* and leader*ship* development processes—and intentional ministries—including evangelism, disciple*ship,* and leader*ship* teams—that work together to cultivate growth, strengthen relation*ships,* and keep the church missionally focused.

Just as a harbor thrives when ships know their course and purpose, the church flourishes when disciples have a clear pathway that directs both inward growth and outward mission. This intentional movement keeps the rhythm of the church healthy and sustainable, guiding people from seekers to disciples who are grounded in Christ the Lighthouse through scripture, prayer, and spiritual practices. Without such direction, disciple*ship* risks becoming aimless, but with it, the harbor of the church becomes a place of transformation where disciples are continually strengthened, aligned, and sent.

Leader*ship* for the Orbital Port

Just as relation*ships* and disciple*ship* are central for becoming a preferred port of call, so too is leader*ship,* as it exhibits missional vitality and Kingdom impact. The leader*ship* of the pastor, the leadership board, and ministry team leaders must be intentionally developed and financially backed.

Chapter 7 reminds us that healthy leader*ship* development results in leader*ship* multiplication. Without the development of both new and existing leaders, the port of call will be either chaotic at best or abandoned at worst. How does your church develop and invest in leaders? What changes need to be considered to have a vital, efficient, and effective port of call?

New Measurements of Vitality

Without gauges and instrumentation, a ship is unable to determine the ship's mechanical soundness, the current levels of essential resources, approaching weather or winds, or if the ship has gotten off course. In Chapter 8, the church was called to examine its current practices for gauging church vitality, missional alignment, and the accuracy and relevance of the measures used.

Each and every port of call needs to measure these essential vitality markers:

- The church's missional effectiveness through growing relation*ships*
- People's growth in their disciple*ship* journey (knowing, loving, following, and behaving more and more like Jesus)
- People's overall well-being, inside and outside the church
- The church's development in identifying and investing in new leaders and the development of existing leader*ship*
- A growing positive impact on the greater community (knowing, serving, connecting) that results in a better community

Which of these vitality markers is your church currently measuring? Is the method of measuring effective, and does it provide the needed information? Is the church leader*ship* willing to make the necessary changes to ensure vitality and effectiveness in all these areas of the church's orbit?

Time to Launch!

You now have the information needed to create your preferred orbital port of call. You have been provided with all the necessary elements (and their descriptions). The potential storms and distractions have been identified to help you steer around them. Possible changes were pinpointed to avoid being drydocked. Sparks of innovation were offered to help you dream God-sized dreams.

While planning and making preparations are wise, don't stay in the harbor too long. Time is of the essence. Ships are sinking at sea! Ships are lost in the turbulent waves of life. Ships are running out of vital supplies as they try to navigate their way to a safe harbor. Act with a sense of urgency! Launch with purpose, vitality, and missional alignment. Don't worry about having everything perfect before you set sail. Course corrections can be made along the way. Godspeed on this important and blessed course for God's preferred future for your port of call.

Don't burn out;
keep yourselves fueled and aflame.
Be alert servants of the Master,
cheerfully expectant.
Don't quit in hard times;
pray all the harder.
Help needy Christians;
be inventive in hospitality.

Romans 12:12 (MSG)

APPENDIX
Additional Resources and Models

The Navigators: "Navigators have helped people around the world bring hope and purpose to others through something we call 'Life-to-Life' disciple*ship*. It's not a program or curriculum; it's more of a commitment to help our friends know Jesus, starting from wherever they are in life. Life-to-Life disciple*ship* has three layers: To know Christ, make him known and help others do the same."[125]

Disciple*ship* in Community: "In today's busy world, many churches struggle to foster authentic community and deep disciple*ship*. Leaders often face challenges in nurturing spiritual growth, leaving congregations disconnected. The Disciple*ship* in Community report, created in partnership with RightNow Media, equips church leaders with research-backed strategies and practical tools to build stronger disciple*ship* and lasting community. Whether you lead a small group, household, or an entire congregation, this resource will help you guide meaningful spiritual transformation."[126]

Family Engagement Core Competencies: A report from the National Association for Family, School, and Community Engagement providing a body of knowledge, skills, and dispositions for family-facing professionals.[127]

---

[125] The Navigators, https://www.navigators.org/.

[126] Barna Group, Discipleship in Community, https://www.barna.com/discipleship-in-community/.

[127] National Association for Family, School, and Community Engagement (NAFSCE), "Family Engagement Core Competencies: A Body of Knowledge, Skills, and Dispositions for Family-Facing Professionals," accessed November 19, 2025, https://nafsce.org/page/corecompetencies.

Three Practice Circles (3P): Jim Henderson and Jim Hancock have created a carefully structured conversation format designed to help people engage across deep differences—in ideology, belief, background—in a way that fosters understanding, safety, and connection. These circles are built around three guiding commitments:

1. I'll be unusually interested in others.
2. I'll stay in the room with difference.
3. I'll stop comparing my best with your worst.[128]

Personal Assessments: Part of helping people grow is offering resources that help them better know and understand themselves, their giftedness, and their talents. Many of the young generations seek out these types of resources. These are great tools that can also be used for purposes of leader*ship* development.

Enneagram: The Enneagram is a personality typing system that describes nine interconnected personality types, each with its own core motivations, fears, and worldview. It's used in various settings like counseling, business, and spiritual growth to help individuals understand themselves and others. The Enneagram is not just about personality traits; it also delves into the underlying motivations that drive behavior.

Meyers-Briggs: The Myers-Briggs Type Indicator (MBTI) is a self-report questionnaire that categorizes individuals into sixteen distinct personality types. It is based on the theory of psychological types developed by Carl Jung and further expanded by Katharine Cook Briggs and Isabel Myers. The MBTI assesses preferences in four dichotomies: Extraversion vs.

---

[128] 3Practices, accessed November 19, 2025, https://3practices.com/.

Introversion, Sensing vs. Intuition, Thinking vs. Feeling, and Judging vs. Perceiving. These preferences combine to form one of the sixteen personality types.

CliftonStrengths: CliftonStrengths, formerly known as StrengthsFinder, is an online assessment developed by Gallup to help individuals identify their unique talents and strengths. It pinpoints an individual's top five strengths from a list of thirty-four themes, categorized into four domains: Strategic Thinking, Relation*ship* Building, Influencing, and Executing. The assessment focuses on what is naturally right with people, helping them understand their potential for building strength in those areas.

APEST: The APEST assessment, also known as the fivefold ministry assessment, is a tool used to identify an individual's unique strengths and expressions within the fivefold ministry model described in Ephesians 4: Apostle, Prophet, Evangelist, Shepherd, and Teacher. It helps individuals understand their ministry style and how they can best contribute to a community or organization. A healthy, vital church is a community of people with a rich blend of all five types. Often, declining churches are missing the Apostles, Prophets, and Evangelists, leaving only the Shepherds and Teachers.

Spiritual Gifts Inventory: Provided by the United Methodist Church Discipleship Ministries, this resource is a series of ninety questions to identify the spiritual gifts of individual disciples.[129]

Compass Points: The Fuller Youth Institute's "Faith Beyond Youth Group" research initiative explored character as the vehicle for both faith longevity and faith vibrancy throughout the week. Their research yielded five compass points to guide

---

129 General Board of Discipleship of The United Methodist Church, "Spiritual Gifts Inventory," accessed November 19, 2025, https://www.umcdiscipleship.org/spiritual-gifts-inventory/en.

the formation of character in young people—cultivating trust, modeling growth, teaching for transformation, practicing together, and making meaning.[130]

When Better Isn't Enough: Evaluation Tools for the 21st Century Church: In this book, author Jill Hudson states, "We must identify new criteria for success, and perhaps even for faithfulness, and hold ourselves accountable to them." Approaching the postmodern era as a tremendous opportunity, Hudson identifies twelve characteristics by which we can measure effective ministry for the early 21st century. Based on those twelve criteria, Hudson has created evaluation tools, "an early measuring stick," to help congregations evaluate their work in this new era.[131]

Scaling Deep: Measures of Possibility, Personhood, and Story: These two articles by Richard Passmore offer his insights: "Scaling deep is about more than numbers or institutional reach; it is about changing hearts and minds, shifting the stories we tell, and nurturing the kind of belonging that can weather storms."[132]

Goodlabs: A consultancy partner that supports nonprofits in understanding and measuring their impact. You'll find articles to better understand this key concept as it pertains to healthy

---

[130] Lewis Center for Church Leadership, "Five Compass Points Guide Character Formation and Lifelong Discipleship for Youth," Leading Ideas, February 28, 2024, https://www.churchleadership.com/leading-ideas/5-compass-points-guide-character-formation-and-lifelong-discipleship-for-youth/.

[131] Jill M. Hudson, *When Better Isn't Enough: Evaluation Tools for the 21st-Century Church* (Herndon, VA: Alban Institute, 2004).

[132] Richard Passmore, "Scaling Deep: Measures of Possibility, Personhood and Story," Sunday Papers – The Supplement (blog), July 9, 2025, https://sundaypapers.org.uk; Richard Passmore, "Scaling Deep – The Place of Lived Experience in Real Change," Sunday Papers – The Supplement (blog), June 27, 2025, https://sundaypapers.org.uk.

churches and vital congregations.[133]

Tearfund.org: A research report from Tearfund.org offers evidence of the impact of church and community transformation in action around the world.[134]

Doing the Math of Mission: This book by Gil Rendle offers theory, models, and new tools for using metrics in ministry. This book also shows how metrics and accountability fit into discernment, goal setting, and ministry strategies.[135]

Presencing Institute: The Presencing Institute offers change-makers innovative tools and methods to lead from the emerging future. Through their proven Theory U approach, they integrate science, collective action, and deep creative processes for systemic transformation. They are a global ecosystem of regional partners in Africa, Asia Pacific, Europe, and the Americas.[136]

---

[133] "Articles," GoodLabs, accessed November 19, 2025, https://www.goodlabs.uk/articles.

[134] Tearfund, "Researching the Impact of CCT: Evidence of the Impact of Church and Community Transformation (CCT) in Action Around the World (2025)," accessed November 19, 2025, https://learn.tearfund.org/en/resources/series/cct-impact-study-series.

[135] Gil Rendle, *Doing the Math of Mission: Fruits, Faithfulness, and Metrics* (Nashville: Abingdon Press, 2014).

[136] Presencing Institute, homepage, https://www.presencing.org/, accessed November 19, 2025.

www.ingramcontent.com/pod-product-compliance
Lightning Source LLC
LaVergne TN
LVHW010055110826
845155LV00028B/359